PRAISE FOR
LITTLE SHIFTS FOR A BIG LIFE

"Big vision, big dreams, big life, big heart, big impact, big results. Everything Nancy Perry does makes you, as the reader, feel big. Vulnerable, raw, truthful, and transformational—this is the essence of Nancy's work. I've known Nancy Perry for over ten years; her gift is making everyone around her better, and this book will undoubtedly make your life better. Through Nancy's wisdom and experiences, *Little Shifts for a Big Life* will inspire you to embrace change and unlock your full potential. Nancy Perry's journey is a testament to the power of small, consistent steps toward living a truly happy and purposeful life."

—**Greg Scheinman,** best-selling author of *The Midlife Male*; speaker, entrepreneur, coach

"In her inaugural book, Nancy Perry delivers page after page of actionable perspectives to make all our days better *now*! I highly recommend *Little Shifts for a Big Life* as a family room perennial, brightening your mind space with fresh thinking, such as 'Don't Take Yourself Personally.' Nancy's voice is funny, honest, and practical. This is a pick-up, read, put-down, and get-after-it type of book! It's a great year-round gift for seekers young and old!"

—**Susanne Conrad,** author *of Get There Now*, founder of Lightyear Leadership

"*Little Shifts for a Big Life* is a powerful, daily guide to help you 'alive' more. Nancy has inspired me personally to do just that. Nancy's Sunday 'sermons,' while leading 100+ of us through a challenging and *very* sweaty yoga practice, have been just the medicine I often need to begin the new week with more aliveness. This book is a collection of her teachings, so that you can live the big, beautiful life you were born to experience. Nancy walks her talk. I consider her a magic maker. You're likely to read her words and make more magic in your own life. I call this: The Nancy Effect."

—**Randi Rubenstein,** founder and owner of Mastermind Parenting

LITTLE SHIFTS FOR A BIG LIFE

Create a Happier, More Intentional Life
Through Choice, Courage, and Commitment

NANCY PERRY

RIVER GROVE
BOOKS

Published by River Grove Books
Austin, TX
www.rivergrovebooks.com

Copyright © 2024 Nancy Perry

All rights reserved.

Thank you for purchasing an authorized edition of this book and for complying with copyright law. No part of this book may be reproduced, stored in a retrieval system, or transmitted by any means, electronic, mechanical, photocopying, recording, or otherwise, without written permission from the copyright holder.

Distributed by River Grove Books

Design and composition by Greenleaf Book Group and Sheila Parr
Cover design by Greenleaf Book Group and Sheila Parr
Cover image © omprakash kumawat97

Publisher's Cataloging-in-Publication data is available.

Print ISBN: 978-1-63299-855-2

eBook ISBN: 978-1-63299-856-9

First Edition

JHP (Love)
EGP (Grace)
BJP (Miracles)
SPEM (Source)
PPD (Support)

CONTENTS

Introduction 1

Part 1: Unconditional Self-Love 7

1. Embrace the Shaky Power of Courage 11
2. Lead Yourself First by Listening 12
3. Explore Your Self instead of Improving Yourself . . . 13
4. Trust the Wisdom of Your Physical Body 15
5. Your Feelings Are Showing, So Start There 16
6. Let Vulnerability Lead 18
7. Find Out Why Everyone Is Right 19
8. Be the Best Version of You 20
9. Celebrate Your Awesome Problems 21
10. Don't Take Yourself Personally 24
11. Let Commitment Free You from Doubt 25
12. Break the Rules You've Made 26
13. Expand What It Means to Be Okay 28
14. Lean In Fiercely 30

Part 2: You've Already Won 33

15. Be Grateful for Your Design 37
16. Take Responsibility for Possibility 38
17. Make Your Conversations Constructive 40
18. Respond Instead of Reacting 42
19. Pause, Listen, and Choose a Useful Perspective . . . 43
20. What Could Go Right? 44

21. Realize You Have Everything You Need 46
22. Practice Faith in the Future 48
23. Only Empower What You Want 50
24. Receive Your Limitless Resources 52
25. Create More of What You Desire 55
26. Find Joy in Discomfort 57

Part 3: Stay in Your Flow 63
27. Create Boundaries with Flow 67
28. Free Yourself from the Drama Cycle 69
29. Believe You Can So You Can 71
30. Let Your Imagination Light the Way 73
31. Transform Your "Buts" to "Ands" 75
32. Practice This Small Thing to Move Forward 77
33. Have a Breakthrough by
    Breaking through Mediocrity 79
34. Focus on Your Purpose and Nothing Else 81
35. Own Your Feminine Leadership 83

Part 4: Choice Is Your Superpower 87
36. Develop a Rule-Breaking Practice 93
37. Your Choices and What They Create 95
38. Choose What You Receive 97
39. Choose to Believe in Peace 99
40. Allow Choice in Others to
    Experience It Yourself 101
41. Take Your 1,440 Opportunities 104

42. Break Free from Pressure. 107
43. Change Yourself to Change Your Life 109
44. Find Freedom in Change 111
45. Choose the Change You Seek 113
46. Celebrate Sunk Costs 115
47. Be Supported by the Power of Enough 117

Part 5: You Are Your Own Fulfillment Center 123
48. Contribute Like a Pro 129
49. Vibrate to Create 131
50. Tell Helpful Stories 133
51. Make It Easy to Change the World 135
52. Expand beyond Right or Wrong 137
53. Be Immune to Dis-courage-ment 139
54. Look for Support Ahead, Not Behind 142
55. Generate Generosity. 143
56. Discover Your Power through Staying 146
57. Own Your Strength through Gentleness 149
58. Try Out the Upgraded Golden Rule 153

Conclusion. 159
About the Author 163

INTRODUCTION

My life doesn't feel like mine. I don't know that it can be mine. I exist to fit in, follow the rules, look good, and receive praise for good performance and looking pretty. But, of course, I also rebel as a part of me knows this is not how my life is supposed to feel. This battle between feeling like I must fit in yet rejecting that I should comply, leads me to have complicated relationships with my emotions, body, peers, food, and pretty much everything.

This describes my feelings at ages nine, twelve, fifteen, eighteen, and twenty-two. At twenty-two years old, I was a college dropout suffering from disordered eating, hiding in overdrinking, and emotionally and spiritually crumbling under the crippling weight of all-consuming shame and blame. That was a far cry from what I felt as a young child: confident, playful, and full of possibility. In my elementary school years, I wanted to be a cashier, a hostess, an astronaut, and the first female president—and I knew that I could. Yet at twenty-two, all I could see was the heartbreak the world would ultimately inflict on all of us. Thankfully, a coworker of mine whom I admired gave me a life-changing invitation to join her for something she thought would help me as much as it had helped her, and I showed up to my first real yoga class.

That yoga class was the turning point for me. The practice began the slow yet rapid process of reawakening the possibility I'd felt as a child. It kickstarted me down a path of reclaiming my own life. My journey started on a yoga mat—reconnecting with the wisdom of my body and the power of my resilient spirit—and expanded into a passion for personal development, leadership, learning, meeting my teacher and mentor, entrepreneurship, and creativity. There are many paths to healing, and this was mine, with the significant first step of reconnecting to my spirit through discovering the importance of loving and partnering with my body.

Today, my life often feels complicated or challenging because I am choosing to express what I have inside of me instead of trying to squash what I have inside of me to meet expectations. This feeling of "hard" is the correct kind of hard, because it requires focus and the discipline to stay connected to my recovered possibility. Creating an authentic life feels like heavy lifting sometimes—moving the doubt, fear, and pressure to conform out of the way. However, this is exactly the kind of heavy lifting that makes me emotionally stronger, just like spending time under tension at the gym or in a yoga pose makes me physically stronger. Practicing making new choices makes things lighter over time.

That first yoga class was seventeen years ago. Since that class, I have opened four yoga studios, named BIG Power Yoga and Out Here Yoga, and started a yoga adventure retreat company, Live Alive Adventures, with my business partners. I have become a leadership coach and am a senior coach at Lightyear Leadership, which is a leadership development company that sources its body of work from spiritual principles and the body's innate intelligence.

My most important roles, however, are those of wife to my amazing husband, Justin, and mother to my two beautiful children, Emerson and Bowen. Both of my pregnancies had their own challenges, and Emerson was born prematurely at twenty-five weeks' gestation, which makes me even more grateful to be their mother today. These last seventeen years have taught me that to make the heavy things light, all I need to do is bring a loving context to the situation, listen within, and trust what I hear. That idea is simple but not always easy, which is why I began to keep a daily record of "useful thoughts." I hope this compilation of useful thoughts that have restored me to myself can do the same for you. Furthermore, I hope that this can be a practical restoration tool for you when you need to recontextualize so you can hear your wisdom.

It is important to remember that love, joy, freedom, and peace are our birthrights and part of our design, meaning they can always be at our fingertips if we know how to access them. My superpower is my ability to choose happiness, forgiveness, and choice. That is your superpower too. I have the blessing of being able to (quite imperfectly!) model and share these truths with my children and my communities, and now I hope to share them with you. I am acutely aware of the gift of this life.

My question for you is this: What if the rest of your life could feel like *your* life?

What if you became an expert at centering and clearing yourself whenever you needed to so you could enjoy the time you have on this earth and contribute your perfect amount of value along the way? What if, instead of overriding or ignoring your feelings in order to get somewhere, there was a new, intuitive, curious, and accepting way to lead yourself and others that was much more fulfilling? If you are interested in feeling, doing, and having these life-changing skills and experiences, you are in the right place.

I've curated some of my many pieces of writing into five parts that I feel are foundational to beginning and sustaining a journey of love for self and others. Each section also includes journaling questions so you can transform the concepts into real changes in your life. Change doesn't happen through getting new information. It happens when we hear or ask ourselves a resonant question.

We will begin with Part 1, "Unconditional Self-Love," exploring what it really means to love ourselves because we can only give as much love to others or receive as much love as we are able to give ourselves. On that foundation, we will move into Part 2, "You've Already Won," and discover how to experience peace in our lives as we ride the inevitable waves of change and emotions. Part 3, "Stay in Your Flow," covers conversations about keeping our connection to unconditional love and peace no matter what so we have the energy to stay focused on what is most important. Part 4 reminds us that we are each born with a superpower we can rely on no matter what comes our way, and that superpower is choice. "Choice Is Your Superpower" sets us up to embrace the freedom that comes with owning our own happiness and contentment in Part 5, "You Are Your Own Fulfillment Center."

If you are starting at a place of frustration, resignation, or burden, know that you can end at a place of peace, inspiration, and freedom.

If you release control and embrace your choice from your values, happiness is guaranteed. You have a choice in who you are being, no matter what happens and no matter the circumstances, and that is your key to happiness and ensured success. This leads you to experience freedom, inspiration, and joy.

Whether at the end of the day or the end of your life, your experience comes down to one thing: Were you the best version of yourself? That is your *only* responsibility. You are free of all the things that you fear. You don't need to spend any time worrying about what someone else might think, whether it will turn out perfectly, or if your decision is the "right" one. People will judge you; things won't go well; decisions will never be certain. This concept is so freeing!

You are ripe to embrace this book and new way of living if you

- know something different is possible, so you feel frustrated with the systems and people around you;
- want to change jobs, focus, or step out of the system, yet you don't see the pathway;
- are ready to share who you really are, yet you are afraid of judgment, misunderstanding, or what other people will think;
- want to experience more meaning and are fearful that in pursuit of something new, you will lose the things that are important to you;
- deeply desire the experience of success but are afraid of failing;
- have a sense there is a new level of abundance available for you if you make a change, yet you are scared of not having enough or being enough; or

- feel excited to contribute, solve problems, and play a bigger game but are afraid to speak up.

Remember: *you* are the solution to the future, the pathway is there, and you are part of creating it. There is no right way. This book will help you remember that at the end of the day and your life, you are so much more than your outcomes—you are free to choose. Essentially, this book will help you deal with the inner critic and the critics around you and restore your ability to make choices.

I have decided to write this book because I know I have a unique perspective to share. I feel that we would live in a much different (better) world if we all took the time to pause, listen in, and choose a perspective that is useful for ourselves and others. I know that we all have wisdom worth listening to within us, so I feel that sharing our wisdom is part of our responsibility as individuals and an essential part of moving things forward for the human race.

With all that being said, I want you to pick up this book in the morning to set the tone for your day, in the middle of the day to correct course, or at the end of the day to convert any challenging experiences into growth with love and self-compassion. My intention is that it is both spiritual and incredibly practical and direct. I want you to feel as if you are connected to something bigger and feel supported in how to deal with the situations right in front of you, no matter what they are. This is a book with principles that are universal and helpful regardless of circumstances.

Part 1

UNCONDITIONAL SELF-LOVE

Our ability to contribute and receive all of the love, joy, abundance, and fulfillment (and all the other good stuff!) we are meant to have is only as great as our capacity to love ourselves. Loving ourselves unconditionally can help us give and receive love unconditionally.

Love is simply one of the best feelings we can experience. We are designed to love, which is why we have more clarity, inspiration, and energy when we do so. In fact, studies show that unconditional love may activate the same areas of our brains as romantic love, potentially releasing oxytocin, a powerful feel-good hormone.[1] We seem designed to give love and receive love, which is why it feels so good. Our bodies have a powerful way of constantly letting us know when we are on the right track, and it's important to learn how to listen.

For instance, when I spend time blaming my husband for something that's happened or judging someone who I believe has wronged me or someone else, I feel a tightness in my throat, heaviness in my whole body, and tension in my neck and jaw. Conversely, I have noticed that when I choose to love or forgive, my body responds with relaxation and warmth. There are times when love is so easy that I don't need to choose it, like when I am hanging out with my closest friends or watching my kids play with such innocence and silliness. The times I need to *choose* love are the times when my first reaction is to go to some variation of victimhood, fear, blame, worry, or doubt. The intensity of the tightness, heaviness, heat, and tiredness I feel in that moment would have me believe that I can't choose love. Yet that is the moment of discipline and the moment of choice.

When I make the *choice* to love, I can feel the ease and spaciousness come back into my body. This is my body confirming I made the correct choice. This peace and alignment are the feelings in which I want to live my life—not to pretend or avoid what's important—so I can enter into the problems I want to help solve with spiritual protection that allows me to go the distance I want to go. When I know that love is something I can stay

---

1 Katherine Wu, "Love, Actually: The Science Behind Lust, Attraction, and Companionship," Harvard Graduate School of Arts and Sciences blog, February 14, 2017, https://sitn.hms.harvard.edu/flash/2017/love-actually-science-behind-lust-attraction-companionship/.

connected to by choice, I don't need to fear the challenges along the way. Love is my anchor back to what is true.

Unconditional love is different from the fleeting "love" we feel in certain relationships—our affinity toward pizza or our favorite meal, or the infatuation we experience over a potential panacea or promised fix-it. Instead, unconditional love is a choice we can make. This love can apply to loving ourselves and to loving others. It is a magnetic force that would change our whole planet if we all chose it. And if you choose unconditional love, it can change your life and the lives of those around you. It all starts with you. With us. The choice to love is especially important when it feels hard to love, for instance, strangers, someone you have considered an enemy, people who have done harm in the world, or even yourself.

In this context, unconditional love is not an emotion. It is not something we need to wait around to feel. It is something we can choose. The ability to choose unconditional love comes from our willingness to surrender to our beautiful human imperfection and our understanding that we cannot control others. Loving transcends agreeing and disagreeing. It transcends the polarity of "right" and "wrong." Choosing to unconditionally love others doesn't mean we need to agree with them or condone their actions. It also doesn't mean we need to trust them or befriend them. In fact, forgiving others and choosing love, especially when we want to judge them, allows us to set powerful boundaries that allow us to thrive. When we forgive and keep our attention on how we respond, we can stay connected to the compassion, curiosity, and understanding within ourselves and get the ultimate say over how we experience our lives.

Choosing unconditional love is a big practice and a whole world to discover. And we can't really practice unconditional love with others until we discover how to do it for ourselves. When we choose to love *ourselves* without condition first and foremost, we can discover how to create a more peaceful and compassionate world. As love is something we are born with and designed to experience, the practice of Unconditional Self-Love begins with releasing expectations and judgments of ourselves—the have-tos, shoulds, can'ts, etc. When we can release the idea that we should be somewhere else or be different than we are, we give ourselves the freedom to meet ourselves as we are and where we are. The key to Unconditional Self-Love is forgiveness—especially when we feel like we don't deserve it. When we choose to love ourselves, we get to learn and grow from past experiences instead of suffering and stagnating.

When we feel good, we do good, and choosing love helps us feel good. When we feel pulled to judge, our task is to choose love instead. There is no "right" journey; there is only the next correct choice to make, which is always available to us, no matter how long we've been making incorrect choices. We can have a fresh start right now—and whenever we need it.

1

EMBRACE THE SHAKY POWER OF COURAGE

You can create more harmony in your own life, and therefore the world, if you are willing to experience how much courage you have within you.

To be empowered means feeling that you can take the steps to remove the discord from your own life. The main thing this takes is courage, and you have as much of it as anyone else on the planet; it's simply a matter of whether you are willing to access it.

Courage often feels shaky, sweaty, nerve-wracking, fluttery, or many other things besides relaxing. To make courage more enticing, picture yourself on the other side of your bravery, feeling the harmony and peace that come from being free.

Harmony is on the other side of the resistance. Empowerment is loving yourself enough to dive in.

2

LEAD YOURSELF FIRST BY LISTENING

To lead someone else, you need to be able to lead yourself because leading starts with listening, and you cannot hear another unless you can listen to yourself.

True leadership is a form of service and is about supporting people in their growth. To support folks, you must be able to support yourself first, eliminating dissonance in your life and taking responsibility for your peace of mind.

Listening to yourself is a discipline in a world full of potential distractions, and it is the only way to truly learn to lead (a.k.a. love) others.

3

EXPLORE YOUR SELF INSTEAD OF IMPROVING YOURSELF

Every night before I put my three-year-old and four-year-old to bed, I tell them, "You are perfect exactly as you are, and you can do anything you want because you are limitless."

We are inherently perfect as we are—the real us, underneath all our habits, heartbreaks, disappointments, coping mechanisms, beliefs, preferences, and opinions. We can call this essential part of us our capital "S" Self. As human beings, inheriting or developing the quirks and patterns that form our personality is inevitable. We can think of this aspect of ourselves as our lowercase "s" self. The relationship between the two is what makes being alive such an enlivening and educational experience.

Since we are both perfect as we are and totally imperfect at the same time, our job is to learn to stay connected to our perfection—which is love—and compassionately and kindly observe what drives us to do what we do. Loving and kind observation with an intention of releasing what doesn't serve us is distinctly different from trying to fix ourselves.

Through our capital "S" Selves, we gain our ability to choose, releasing what no longer helps us and giving us permission to try new things. This nonjudgmental Self-exploration can allow us to notice how we feel when we make shifts and changes, allowing us to create lives we enjoy and contribute to others. If we can take this on as a lifelong practice that has no end goal, destination, or "fix-it" attached to it, our evolution can become an adventure versus something to get right.

4

TRUST THE WISDOM OF YOUR PHYSICAL BODY

Your body does not know how to lie to you and is always speaking to you. It is a blessing to have such an honest partner, and, of course, it sometimes feels inconvenient when you would rather run the show on your own.

If you listen to (a.k.a. feel without labeling) your body, you can sense what it feels like when it doesn't like what you're thinking or doing and what it feels like when it does like what you're thinking or doing. This is incredibly useful because your body does not have an agenda, and your mind often does. Your mind's agenda can tempt you or trick you into overriding what is needed now in favor of what will give you instant gratification. Your body also knows the difference between instant gratification and long-term fulfillment.

While your mind will give you reasons to ignore your body, it is essential to listen to it if living a life sourced from wisdom is your goal. Wisdom is the only thing that can guarantee us peace of mind and contentment for the long haul. So make your body your best friend as you navigate your day and your life.

5

YOUR FEELINGS ARE SHOWING, SO START THERE

The transformation of anything must start from the inside—of you.

Things only transform in the presence of truth. So if you're trying to change any external circumstance and you have underlying resentment, resignation, frustration, or limiting belief toward the situation, you will eventually undermine your own efforts.

As soon as things get challenging, as they surely will with anything worth transforming, your true feelings will start to show. Any feelings like the ones listed here will be revealed and will thwart your intention in its tracks, potentially even producing the opposite result from what you were looking for. Things don't transform in the presence of fear and reaction; they retreat and contract.

It requires more than just a good intention to transform something. It will take examining the way you feel about and perceive the people and situations you want to create change with, including yourself. It takes choosing faith, responsibility, and forgiveness over doubt, resignation, and reaction.

If you're looking to cause a positive shift in a situation, in a relationship, or in your own behavior, start with your feelings.

When you connect to feelings of compassion, acceptance, curiosity, commitment, and faith, you will be able to remain yourself when things get challenging, which will provide the truth and support to change.

6

LET VULNERABILITY LEAD

Connection arises in the presence of generosity. True vulnerability is the practice of sharing our own human experience, which is different from sharing our opinions and grievances.

We often victimize ourselves and blame others to avoid feeling our own emotions and body sensations. The problem with this is that it blocks us from true connection because connection is a feeling.

Sharing what we are feeling, what we are learning, and what we are cultivating is vulnerability.

7

FIND OUT WHY EVERYONE IS RIGHT

No one is ever wrong from their perspective.

If you want to change someone's mind, you have to start by doing your best to understand what they see from their perspective. They literally have a different point of view from yours, so they are seeing something different from what you are seeing. Only once you can imagine what they are seeing does a useful dialogue become possible.

They're not wrong, and you're not wrong. You have two different perspectives, and each is the reality.

8

BE THE BEST VERSION OF YOU

It is almost impossible to be the best at something in the world. There is always going to be someone who does it a little "better." There is going to be someone richer, fitter, smarter, funnier, prettier, kinder, taller, more talented, etc. Even if it were possible to be the absolute best out of all people, there would be no way of knowing who the winner was. Besides, any work done with the main intention of beating others will not fulfill you at a soul level.

There is, though, one thing that you can be the best at, and that is being you. There is literally no one else who can do it and no one else who could discover how to do it. So why not take all your energy and power and have some fun being the best version of yourself?

9

CELEBRATE YOUR AWESOME PROBLEMS

I hope you get to deal with some awesome problems today.

Your life will never be problem free. To be alive means to have problems to solve. The question is, How awesome are your problems? If you're sick of dealing with the same boring problems, get yourself some bigger and better ones.

To be able to upgrade your problems, start practicing being grateful for the problems you have rather than seeing them as something to be stopped by. When your car gives you trouble, be grateful you have a car and the opportunity to deal with the problems that come with that. As hard as it may seem when you find yourself upset about the election results, could you practice being grateful for a flawed yet impactable government system? When you find yourself dissatisfied with the appearance of your body, could you try being grateful that you have a living and breathing body and the opportunity to deal with the problems that come with that? If all else fails, simply practice the gratitude of being alive and having the opportunity to deal with the problems that come with that.

Gratitude is the foundation of receiving, so practicing gratitude as you move through challenges can help you receive the help you need, from within and without, to overcome what would have once stopped you from stepping into a new level of expression, contribution, and success.

When you can stop being taken out by your current problems, this opens up space for new and bigger problems that may seem more worth your time. No matter what your current problems are, there are new and better ones available to you.

Here are some things to consider making your problems:

- Receiving feedback from people who care about what you are up to
- Having a team or family who look to you for leadership, which guarantees you will disappoint people
- Paying more taxes because you are in a higher income bracket
- Having a large percentage of the general population judge you because you are making a real difference in a social matter that matters to you
- Feeling doubt from people because you have a brand-new idea you are going all in on
- Being in the uncertainty and possibility of launching a new project that could fail
- Finding funds to provide relief to millions, thousands, hundreds of people—or one person
- (Add yours too!) _____

_____

What do you want to be grateful to have the opportunity to deal with? Today, start to be grateful for the problems that you do have so you can make way for more interesting ones.

10

DON'T TAKE YOURSELF PERSONALLY

When you feel good and life feels good, it can be easy to remember that you are a divine being, perfect at your core. When life feels hard or you aren't at your best, you might start to doubt yourself.

Doubt, fear, sadness, frustration, and all those unpleasant things will certainly be a part of your life experience—in some seasons more than others. They will be for all of us. Do not take these things personally, meaning that under all that stuff, there is a whole, perfect, eternal being that cannot be changed. This part of you, which is love, can hold space for you as your human self discovers its way.

11

LET COMMITMENT FREE YOU FROM DOUBT

You don't need to trust in the outcome; you need to trust in yourself. You will experience many successes and many failures, and that's normal, if not preferable. What will get you through the inconsistencies of life is your *commitment* to your success, and your success is knowing you acted with personal integrity.

If you know what you stand for and who you are committed to being, you can always trust yourself to succeed in the long term.

You don't need to control the outcome; you need to trust in yourself. Success doesn't have to do with the results that someone else sees; it has to do with knowing you did what was essential to you. When you feel the (sometimes very strong) pull to ignore what you value, this is how you know you have an extraordinary opportunity to increase your self-trust. Your freedom from that pull and your freedom in the long term come when you refuse to ignore your wisdom anymore, no matter how uncomfortable it feels.

12

BREAK THE RULES YOU'VE MADE

Many of the rules that govern your everyday behaviors and limit your experiences are made up by you.

- I *can* do this. I *can't* do that.
- I *can* only be successful in this field. I *can't* risk failing in this new area.
- I *am allowed* to eat this. I *am not allowed* to enjoy this.
- It *is appropriate* to talk about this with these people. I *should* keep my mouth shut about this topic around these people.

You might have made your rules up along the way in reaction to what you observed growing up, or they may be rules you unknowingly inherited from others. If you look, these rules are everywhere in your life, deeply ingrained to the point you don't even see them as rules; you see them as facts. The good news is that all it takes to start making new rules for yourself is to realize you can break the ones you have set for yourself, along with the willingness to experience the discomfort that comes from creating something new.

If you're reading this, you're likely incredibly blessed to live in a place with freedoms that provide you with boundless opportunities and the possibility to be self-expressed. Realizing and owning how free you truly are can be confronting. You have full responsibility for what you do and don't do. It takes courage to break rules that feel real to you and no longer serve you.

Next time you find yourself feeling stuck or unfulfilled, look for the rule that you are following that it is time to break. One of the most common rules that many of us need to break is the rule that it is not okay to ask for help, that we need to do it all, or that we need to have all the answers on our own. When we notice this rule at play, our job is to go ask for help and experience the freedom that comes from breaking an oppressive, self-enforced rule.

While it takes energy to create a new pathway, remember: anything you do contributes to the likelihood of others doing it too. You might just open up a new door for someone else.

13

EXPAND WHAT IT MEANS TO BE OKAY

The less we are upset and thrown off by life, the greater the impact we can make. If we lose it when things don't go our way, we will only be able to engage with things that are predictable. This is problematic because the most fulfilling things in life are unpredictable. If we get upset when others disagree with us or see things from a different point of view, we won't be able to collaborate with others, contribute or be contributed to, or enjoy deeply loving relationships. If we throw our self-worth out the window when we fail, we won't be able to take risks, create meaningful things, or grow. Most importantly, if we fear the emotions of loss or disappointment, we won't be able to fully love. All love involves heartbreak.

As we learn to practice openheartedness in the face of uncertainty, disagreement, failure, frustration, disappointment, or heartache, we become resilient and unstoppable. Imagine the ocean. It is fluid, accepting, and so powerful that raindrops do not upset it. It flows with, creates with, and even absorbs whatever comes its way. The ocean is expansive and is always okay. Our work is the same—not to stop the rain or the tides but rather to expand enough that we know we will be whole.

You have an important contribution to make. However, you won't be able to make it if you think you aren't okay just because someone doesn't agree with you or because life feels hard. What if everything didn't have to be perfect for you to be okay? What if raindrops and waves are just part of it? If you can continually expand your threshold of what it means to be okay, you can continue to expand your contribution.

14

LEAN IN FIERCELY

Our spirits, souls, and bodies love the feeling of being all in. To be all in means believing in yourself and everything you commit to 100 percent. On all the levels mentioned, we can sense when we doubt ourselves or the other person or thing. The results of that doubt can be detrimental, either leading to self-sabotage or "other-sabotage" at a gross or subtle level.

Being all in can feel frightening because it takes away your escape hatch. However, giving yourself over entirely to your worthiness and a big possibility is the only way you can fully know yourself.

If you cannot believe in the other person or thing, your work is either to choose to believe or realize it's time to find what you believe in. And to discover that thing, you must believe in yourself. It all starts there.

To trust in yourself does not mean that you are certain you will always make the "right" decisions or that things will always go according to your plan. To trust yourself means to humbly accept that you were designed with the ability to sense your correct next response, whether things are going as expected or feel like they are falling apart. To trust yourself means you release trying to do what you are not designed to do: control outcomes.

You cannot control what others do. You cannot control what others think. You cannot even control what you think. When you have the courage to stop wasting your energy doing things you cannot do, you can surrender to the beauty of your ability to respond. Your wise voice within will speak when you are listening.

To know what to be all in on, be all in with the present moment.

Unconditional Self-Love

PART 1 JOURNALING PROMPTS

- Imagine you considered love your most important job and priority. How would that change the way you treat the three people in your life who challenge you the most?
- What would you be able to change in your life if you gave yourself permission to be 100 percent direct and 100 percent loving, both with yourself and someone else, in the area where you have felt most stuck?
- Where is a place that you have felt energy building up? Where have you been avoiding it rather than leaning into it? What might you experience if you were willing to move straight into that energy with love rather than continuing to resist?
- Where have you been prioritizing someone else's preferences or opinions over what you know to be true? If you prioritized honoring yourself, what do you sense you would be able to experience or accomplish?
- How do you sense your life would shift if you devoted all your energy and power to having fun being the best version of *you*, not the best version of anyone else?

Part 2

YOU'VE ALREADY WON

I heard that my teacher's teacher, Dorothy Wood Espiau, once said, "The only way you can lose is to forget that you've already won."

Almost all wisdom traditions will teach you that you already have the divine within you, and all valuable practices of transformation exist to help you get all the extra stuff that's not you off so you can clearly see that divine part of yourself. This understanding has completely transformed my life as a recovered prover and hider.

When I was in grade school, I thought that if I could keep securing praise and accolades for my achievements, I would be able to maintain my status of "good enough." When I was in middle school, I thought that if I could get the approval of the popular kids and cutest boys, I would finally be safe from rejection. In high school, I felt that if I could be thin enough and therefore pretty enough, I would finally be loved, embraced, and supported the way I desperately wanted to be. And, unfortunately, by the time I (somehow) got to college, I was so deep into my unwinnable game of keeping up facades that I had no idea how to win at what is actually important: knowing myself and staying connected to my innate, unchangeable divine perfection. I had no idea who I was.

My eighteen-year-old self was in so much pain. My soul ached from years of neglect. I had spent so much time and energy calculating how to be, what to consume, what to avoid, and how to protect myself, and none of it had worked. As a last-ditch effort to control my world, I doubled down on avoiding anything and everything uncomfortable. This included my classes in school, being honest with my friends and family about what I was going through, and being honest with myself. I also doubled down on numbing myself with things that gave me perceived comfort, like alcohol, food, and self-pity. My obsession with hiding from the big feelings of life eventually resulted in me failing out of college and lying to my parents and almost everyone else. Unsurprisingly, I believed that lying to others was how I could protect myself from their judgment. I know now that this attempt at "protecting" myself from what others might think about me was the problem all along. In so many ways, I was taught that the way to be happy was to fit in, which is the opposite of truly belonging.

The time that followed my premature departure from college was the darkest time of my life. It was a period full of regret, resentment, shame, resignation, fear—you name it. I look back now and see just how harmful it was to believe that I had to earn or prove something to "win" at the game of life. It was exhausting and honestly could have killed me. However, I am now so grateful because I would not have eventually found yoga and everything my practice brought along with it.

My first yoga teacher said, "You are a whole, complete, and perfect divine being." It was such a foreign concept to me, as my whole life, I had learned that I was imperfect and there was something about me to fix. But, as alien as the concept was, it resonated deeply. Profoundly, I ended up making my whole life about helping others remember that truth.

We are all already perfect, and that includes you. Our wholeness does not give us a free pass to be jerks or abdicate our responsibility to evolve into our best selves and contribute. Instead, it means that we can take our focus off what other people think or expect and turn our attention inward to align our thoughts and actions with what is most true to us. True personal responsibility is the opposite of selfishness. When we do this kind of inner work from a place of remembering that we have already won, we will automatically be inspired to serve others as a part of our authentic self-expression.

When you want another way to connect to the part of you that is already victorious and cannot lose, I hope the writings in this section can help you with that.

15

BE GRATEFUL FOR YOUR DESIGN

Some not-wonderful things have likely happened in your past. They certainly have in mine. These were not things that "happened for a reason," things we would hope to happen again, or things we would wish on someone else.

While we need not feel grateful for the actual events themselves, it's entirely possible (and optimal) to be thankful for how we have grown as a result. We were beautifully and intelligently designed to glean value out of any circumstance if we choose to. It is an insurance plan built into our humanness—because we can't always control what happens, we were created to have a choice about how we respond and who we become. No person, place, or thing can take that power away from us.

Appreciating your divine design's magic can give you your power back.

16

TAKE RESPONSIBILITY FOR POSSIBILITY

When things happen that we don't expect, especially things we weren't hoping would happen, our tendency can often be to put our attention on what's gone wrong or on the negative impacts of the circumstance.

While keeping our eyes open for possible negative impacts and handling them can be helpful, it is only sometimes beneficial to put *most* of our attention on them. Whatever we put our attention on and think about is what dictates our actions. Therefore, we miss out on possibilities if we focus primarily on the negative.

We don't cause bad things to happen simply by thinking about them; however, we limit the possibility of beautiful things happening when we don't take the time to picture them and see that they *could* happen. To help facilitate a positive result in response to a setback, we must first believe that the positive outcome is possible. Once we think it is possible, we can focus on that possibility and build up the energy, inspiration, and courage to nudge that possibility toward reality. We will only take that action if we see that something good and surprising is possible.

When my daughter was born more than three months early, we found out that she had suffered a severe brain bleed either during or shortly after her birth. Along with this news came the possibility that her brain would not be able to absorb cerebrospinal fluid and that she might need at least one brain surgery, if not multiple. In the following days, weeks, and months, we watched to see what would happen. During this period of uncertainty, I would start to sink down into worry about my daughter's future; I would fear the next piece of bad news; I would blame myself for giving birth prematurely; I would express frustration with our medical teams for not having more answers. It felt so easy to stay in that space because I had every good reason to do so if I wanted to. However, I knew that was not the place to see possibility from.

Because I was blessed enough to have the tools my teachers had given me, I was able to choose to focus on who I wanted to be rather than what was happening to me. Shifting my focus again and again, I was able to continually redirect my energy toward being a loving presence for my daughter and a present and curious listener and researcher. The decision to shift as many times as I needed gave me the clarity to learn how to do everything I could to help her thrive, including making bold requests and asking courageous questions that I would not have if I had been stuck in my victim mode. I know that part of why my daughter is doing so well today, five years later, is because I focused on what was possible—most importantly when I felt like everything was wrong.

Especially when life challenges us, our work is to focus on what is possible versus what our reactive minds may tell us we should fear in the future. Make this simple choice (again and again) to support yourself in having a shot at creating the results you want and being at ease in the present moment.

17

MAKE YOUR CONVERSATIONS CONSTRUCTIVE

Your conversations' quality determines your life's quality because your conversations determine what you create.

If you need to win by being right or proving that someone else is wrong, you are in the wrong conversation. This type of "communication" distracts you from what is essential and what your time is meant for because it causes more division, blame, and fault.

Instead of making your conversations about assigning blame, consider making them about learning how to grow in your ability to collaborate and bring out the best in people. Recently, I was having a conversation with an employee about why something didn't happen that was supposed to happen. Instead of focusing on the "mistake," I asked if she wanted any support in her work so she could feel even more successful. She recommended that we have a brief one-on-one each week when I can specifically offer her appreciation and validation in her work and role so she can notice the successes she is already having. This suggestion has been one of my favorite parts of my week and has led to not only deeper collaboration and partnership between the two of us but has also inspired other similar structures in our company as well.

When you find yourself in a conversation, either in your head or with someone else, that is counterproductive to what you want to be up to, stop it. Stop having that conversation, and start asking questions that lead the conversation in the direction of what is truly best for everyone. It's that simple.

How wonderful that you get to choose what you talk about and what you don't.

18

RESPOND INSTEAD OF REACTING

To respond is to choose. To react is to have something else choose for you.

I have never met anyone who claims they *want* to feel frustrated, agitated, angry, doubtful, mean, or rude. I know all these negative experiences arise when we react to life rather than responding to it.

You were given the gift by your creator, the powerful energy that brought our humanness into existence, to choose how you respond to life. In fact, this freedom to choose is the superpower that makes you human. No matter what happens or what has happened, you have the choice now to take a few deep breaths and respond in a way that makes you proud and feel the way you want to feel about yourself.

What would make you prouder? Staying angry or forgiving? Gossiping or sharing what you are grateful for? Withholding or sharing generously? Not only did your creator design you to choose, but it also designed you to feel your best when you love others. To respond to life is to love.

19

PAUSE, LISTEN, AND CHOOSE A USEFUL PERSPECTIVE

The only useful way to respond to someone or something is with love—especially when you don't understand the person or situation. Love is the ultimate mountain to stand on because it provides you with the power to see things from a higher perspective, one that allows you to see the whole picture even though you can't see the details.

When you feel pulled to react with anger, fight darkness with darkness, or argue about who is right, that energy is unlikely to get you what you actually want, which (I bet) is love. The only thing that will get you love is responding with love, which sometimes means not responding at all.

When you feel the tension of reactivity pulling you quickly away from yourself, pause, listen in, and choose the only perspective that has the possibility of helping everyone. Instead of viewing love as a feeling you need to wait around and feel, view it as a choice you can make that can help you see options you wouldn't have otherwise seen; options that will leave you a lot prouder than the ones you would have taken from a state of reaction. Choosing gives you your power back. You don't need to wait for anything.

20

WHAT COULD GO RIGHT?

Your resistance doesn't want you to see all the things that could go right because you might be inspired to take action.

When making decisions, we tend to focus on all the things that could go wrong. We also do this when getting out of bed in the morning or looking to the week or year ahead.

While it is essential to be aware of the obstacles you may face, focusing on adverse outcomes is your resistance hard at work trying to keep you small and comfortable.

The resistance of others doesn't want you to see all the things that could go right because then you might disrupt the status quo and force a change, moving everyone out of their comfort zones. It is vital to know that resistance is loud, it is forceful, and it will do everything it can to keep you from growing.

Fortunately, you're more powerful than your resistance. All it takes is noticing and making a new choice. Start noticing when your voice of opposition obsesses over what could go wrong. Laugh at the voice a little. When you can point to it, identify it, and most importantly, take it lightly, it starts to lose its power, and you reconnect to your authentic self.

Now, start to focus on what could go right. Start to focus on what you could contribute, the change you could make, the people you could impact, how much fun you could have, and how much you could grow. Finally, please focus on the victory it would be for you to begin making decisions based on what could go right while considering obstacles instead of making decisions based on what could go wrong and underestimating yourself and others.

21

REALIZE YOU HAVE EVERYTHING YOU NEED

What if you knew you were being taken care of, and all you had to do was demonstrate you knew that by taking action? How would that change the choices you make? What if what you're lacking or your bad luck was only perceived?

What would you permit yourself to consider if you knew you had what you needed and knew you were taken care of, loved, supported, and already perfect?

When I allow myself to consider that I have what I need, that I am taken care of, that I am loved and supported, and that I am already perfect, life becomes a lot less stressful. It becomes less stressful because I get my creativity back.

Just as an experiment, imagine you do have everything you need, and you are totally taken care of. Notice how that feels in your body. Now, allow yourself to brainstorm at least thirty things you might be courageous enough to try if you knew you were abundant and safe.

Did you see any ideas you hadn't previously seen? Creativity and opportunity emerge and thrive in the space of enoughness, and you are already enough at your essence. Enough is a frequency to tune into, not something you eventually earn. If you tune in, it will change your whole life.

Is it possible I don't have what I need, that I'm not taken care of, that people are, in fact, out to get me, and that I am inherently flawed? Sure, I guess so. Yet believing this doesn't support me in living the kind of life I want, so I choose to believe something that makes me feel better and act better.

22

PRACTICE FAITH IN THE FUTURE

If there's an area of your life where doubt, fear, or disappointment are keeping you from moving forward, or if these things are keeping you from enjoying your day and life, consider starting to act "as if" and offering yourself some valuable options.

Ask yourself, "What would I do and who would I be if I had just a little faith in the future?" You may already notice yourself starting to shift.

The upgrade from there is asking yourself, "What would I do and who would I be if I had a strong faith in the future?"

The most powerful question to ask yourself for support in shifting into what is possible for you would be, "What would I do and who would I be if I had total faith in the future?"

Let yourself answer these questions with multiple answers. Keep asking, "What else?"

Now that you have many options on the table, you have a choice. Which of these options feel like they will offer you just the right amount of growth so you will be stepping to the edge of your comfort zone yet not to the point of panic? Take these steps.

It's often easier to take baby steps to get somewhere new. Sometimes, we realize it is time for a change and take a giant leap. More frequently, though, we stay in a place that doesn't serve us anymore because we are afraid to jump. The good news is that you don't have to wait there anymore.

Ask yourself, "What you would do 'if?'" You are capable of even more than you think, so act "as if" you are.

23

ONLY EMPOWER WHAT YOU WANT

You'll find whatever you seek out. Our hunger for drama is why there will never be a day when the newscasters say, "Nothing happened to talk about today." As long as we keep seeking it out, it will be there for us to find.

If we want to take our attention off the lower-road conversations in our lives and put it on something more useful, we must choose to stop listening to and engaging with those conversations. Our job is to acknowledge that we are keeping these conversations in place by engaging with them and giving them our time and energy. When we stop engaging with the unuseful, it will disappear or at least quiet down and become less impactful. Removing ourselves doesn't mean becoming ignorant and avoiding problems; bringing the same harmful energy isn't going to create a new, better thing. Only a higher frequency will create a higher thing. Only permit yourself to spend your energy on something if you are going to be productive, proactive, and take the highest road available.

It takes conscious effort, courage, and discipline to say no to the pull of drama. The power of the temptation of instant "gratification" is why most of us get caught up in nonsense without even realizing it. A world free of the conversations that pull us down and enlivened by the ones that inspire us won't happen by accident. This shift can only happen person by person, choice by choice. Start with your world and the conversations you are a part of.

24

RECEIVE YOUR LIMITLESS RESOURCES

Your resources are unlimited. You were given the ability to envision, and you were given access to all you needed to be able to fulfill that vision and more.

Imagine you found out you had unlimited means available to do what you know you are meant to do, and all you must do is be creative in how you find them. Now, for the sake of possibility, are you willing to consider that you don't have to imagine this reality because it might be the truth? If you are willing to consider this, take a pause and brainstorm a list of ten or more (ideally thirty!) ideas for how you might acquire the resources you desire. Who could you talk to? What could you research? What opportunities have you not fully considered because of a limiting belief? Let the bad ideas come out too; they might turn out to be the best ones.

It may be true that your supplies are limitless, and nothing can take them away from you if you are willing to get uncomfortable and begin releasing your old, habitual ways of relating to the world you live in. Could it be that the main obstacles blocking you from the things you need to be able to create are your doubt and addiction to comfort?

With this possibility in mind, it is likely that changing what you say to yourself about the world, other people, and yourself is your most leveraged move because what you say either creates or cuts off opportunities. And of course, your words can be your greatest enemy if you use them to stay the same.

Some possible language upgrades:

Change: "There's not enough; even if there were, I wouldn't know how to get it."
To: "Everything I need is available, and I allow myself to be creative and brave in finding it."

Change: "I can't; it's too hard and not meant for me."
To: "This obstacle is a springboard to launch me into what is next, as each challenge provides me with expansive learnings and strength that I invest in my future. Only good comes to me."

Change: "There's not enough to go around. If it goes away, it won't come back."
To: "The more I give, the more I have to offer. My supply is limitless because generosity begets generosity."

Change: "Life is hard. Some people are lucky, and some people aren't."
To: "Blessings come to me when I have faith and remember I am blessed because receiving is directly correlated with gratitude."

Change: "What if they say no?"
To: "Rejection is protection, and I use every no to guide me to the next opportunity."

The preceding are examples. I recommend taking the time now to create the antidotes to your biggest blocks by playing with phrases and sensing what resonates with you. Feel in your body which words bring you peace and energy, and follow them. One thing is sure: it will take something new to get something new. Your imagination is your ally in generating limitless abundance.

25

CREATE MORE OF WHAT YOU DESIRE

When you don't feel like yourself, please don't worry. Instead, be kind to yourself, and do something about it.

Whatever you put your attention on you create more of. If you worry about the feeling you are experiencing, you will perpetuate it. What takes more energy and discipline is lovingly noticing how you feel and then giving yourself what you need. It will likely be way more helpful to bring your attention off what you don't want and put it on what you do want.

Once you know how you want to feel, support yourself in moving in that direction. It could be simply going outside. It could be exercising. It could be calling your mom or your friend. It could be reaching out to your therapist or taking a big step in your mental health self-care. It could be forgiving yourself. It could be apologizing to someone else. It could be saying a prayer or remembering to be grateful. Maybe listening to your favorite song helps you shift.

Shifting from feeling not like yourself to feeling back to normal is an essential skill to develop and can become quite simple if you stop beating yourself up for needing to do it. Experiencing thoughts of doubt, fear, and resistance is part of being a human being, so there is no need to worry. Our work is to be responsible and love ourselves enough to take steps to allow the light in again.

While self-reflection and getting to the root cause can be critical, this process will be much more helpful from a place of curiosity and compassion. Worrying is like praying for what you don't want and has the power to pull you back to where you started.

Especially don't worry about worrying. Instead, notice and do what you can. And what you can do is put your attention on responding with love, no matter the situation.

26

FIND JOY IN DISCOMFORT

"Normal" is comfortable, which is why we gravitate toward it. We all need a little normal in our lives. It makes us feel relaxed and safe, which is essential to our well-being. However, normal has its limitations.

New and better don't exist in the world of the ordinary. Growth doesn't live inside normal; as humans, we feel our best when we grow in all areas of our lives. Our ability to love, our ability to serve and contribute, our relationships, our careers, and even our bank accounts will all likely grow if we commit to experiencing appropriate discomfort at the appropriate times. If we constantly seek comfort, we won't grow like we are meant to, even if things are already great.

New and better can be found in what we perceive as uncommon, unusual, and extraordinary. Because these things aren't a part of our every day, they are inherently uncomfortable. If we seek to grow, thrive, and contribute, it is our work to seek out or fully embrace awkward, intense, or unnerving opportunities.

The unknown and the new can be stressful, confusing, and frustrating. However, our creator designed us to be able to experience and navigate them so we can evolve. Even better, we are designed to be able to stay with the uncomfortable things until they become comfortable, stay with the hard until it becomes easy, stay with the new until it becomes old, and stay with the unfamiliar until it becomes routine.

Sometimes new and uncomfortable lasts a few minutes. Sometimes a few years. It will become normal if we welcome, allow, and embrace it. Having expanded what feels normal for us, we will have a new level of choice and creativity available to us. We will feel more comfortable and more able to be and express ourselves. We can contribute more and feel more connected. More ease only comes from being willing to be uneasy for a bit.

Think about holding a balancing yoga pose on one leg as you feel the heat in your calf muscle intensify. Or think about the burn you feel in your biceps as you increase your reps at the gym and commit to discovering how many you can actually do versus how many your mind thinks you can do. When you notice the difference between the sensations in your body and what your mind is saying about those sensations, you can trust yourself to work right to the edge of your threshold—neither pushing too far nor giving up too easily. You can practice staying connected to your body and your intuition as you expand your ability to ask for what you want at work, express your love and dreams to your partner, embark on a creative and vulnerable endeavor like writing, or interview or audition for a new opportunity. Right on the other side of the push is the pause, where you can rest in the known again.

Enjoy normal. Then. seek out the uncomfortable. The more unfamiliar you are willing to feel, the more at ease you'll eventually feel.

You've Already Won

PART 2 JOURNALING PROMPTS

- Choose a circumstance from the past that you still feel frustrated or constrained by. To let your spirit transform your pain into power, articulate what you have gained or how you have become stronger as a result of this situation. Remember, owning what you have gained does not condone what happened.

- Choose an area of your life where you feel like you have been experiencing setbacks that are leading to disappointment, failure, or frustration. What if you were to see that area as an opportunity to expand your ability to stay connected to possibility? What would you focus on then? What actions might that open up?

- Where in your life do you currently feel pulled to nitpick, blame, or point out what is wrong? What is the possibility you could focus on instead? What different actions could you take, or what conversations could you have inside of this new context?

- Where have you stopped yourself from acting or moving toward a dream because you believe there is not enough time, money, skill, approval, or support? What if there were enough, and you simply had to move forward and trust the process to receive it? What would be the first three actions you would take?

- Where are you not asking for what you want because you are certain your request will be declined? What if the answer could actually be "yes"? Are you willing to let an imaginary "no" block you from asking for what you want?

- What if you had no problem at all hearing the answer "no"? What would you ask for that you haven't asked for? What would you offer that you haven't offered?
- Choose an area where you feel doubtful, overwhelmed, or resigned, and ask yourself the following:
  - *What would I do and who would I be **if** I had a little faith in the future?*
  - *What would I do and who would I be **if** I had a strong faith in the future?*
  - *What would I do and who would I be **if** I had total faith in the future?*
- What do you say you *don't* want, yet you are spending your energy on it? Where could you spend your energy instead that would support you in moving toward what you know would truly benefit you?
- What is the most impactful limiting belief you have, and how is it blocking you from moving toward what is important to you? What is the uplifting total opposite of this belief? It is likely that this is closer to the truth. Would you be willing to try this new belief on for a day or a year? If so, what might you do differently?
- Where in your life do you wish things were different? How might those instances block you from seeing other opportunities within your reach?

- Is there an area of your life where you are so hard on yourself that you're not even able to *be* yourself? How would your life change if you committed to never beating yourself up again for making a mistake, how others perceive you, or things out of your control? How would the people in your life benefit?
- Where have you been unwilling to evolve or try something new? Could you practice being uncomfortable in order to discover a potential new level of power or expression?

Part 3

STAY IN YOUR FLOW

In the yoga world, the term vinyasa is often referred to as the practice of linking movement with breath and is often called "flow." However, a friend, teacher of mine, and fellow yoga teacher Gioconda Parker shared a definition of vinyasa that resonated with me. She shared that vinyasa means to "place with intention." This opened the realization for me that when we are in true flow, we are simply moving ourselves with focused intention through our lives and the world.

This is an important distinction because in this context, flowing is different from drifting. When I am drifting in my life, I am allowing the circumstances of my life to dictate my emotional state. I am letting the predictability of the past limit what I see possible today and am making choices that seem the most familiar instead of the most powerful. When I am flowing, I am intently focused on what I want to feel and create. I see today's circumstances as vehicles to help me get where I want to go and am willing (even excited) to experience discomfort to help me grow. I much prefer the feeling of being in my flow to being in a drift, even though the former can take lots of energy and the latter takes almost none. This next section is about having the discipline to stay in *your* flow versus drifting and "going with the flow."

After I failed college, I condemned myself to a future of low-paying, unfulfilling jobs and a life of rebellion—as a reaction and not as a choice. The traumatic experiences of living with undiagnosed and therefore untreated eating disorders, lying my way through my early adulthood and the shame of feeling broken, abusing my body with alcohol and other forms of self-sabotage, scraping by and barely making it paycheck to paycheck, and generally feeling isolated and alone as a human being further ingrained in me that I was inherently broken. I knew for a fact that I, a college dropout, would never know enough. I knew for a fact that I would never be reliable or brave enough to see something through. I knew for a fact that I was a disappointment and people would always leave me. I also knew I could never make money or generate real wealth because I was horrible with money and totally irresponsible. It was a pretty miserable reality to live in. And it felt like just that: a reality.

A few months into my yoga practice, I was holding a pose (called extended side angle) for what felt like a hundred breaths. My hamstrings and quadriceps felt like they were going to incinerate from the inside out. I was dripping sweat from head to toe, and my heart was pumping so strongly that I could feel the pulsation in my jaw. I was focused on keeping my breath smooth and steady. Suddenly, I heard my mind clearly say, "There is no way I can do this." Yet there I was, doing it. My mind was saying one thing, and my body was doing something different. This was a breakthrough moment for me. What else was my mind telling me that was untrue? I realized, in that moment, the answer to that question: almost everything.

I wish I could say that I left that class and was immediately liberated from all my limiting thinking. I was not, but that day, I began my journey of learning to discern the difference between the voice of doubt and the voice of my true self. I slowly and surely gave myself permission to open to possibility again. I re-enrolled in college and received excellent grades. I started to see myself as a leader at the restaurant I worked at and began to wonder where else I might be able to contribute. I said yes to doing yoga teacher training and finished it. I began to pay back debts and save for things that were important to me, including a big move across the country from Philadelphia to Houston. Choice by choice, I felt more like myself, more in my flow. I was breaking free from the drift.

My biggest swing for freedom came in 2011, when I felt deeply pulled to open a yoga studio in Houston, where folks could have transformational experiences like the ones I'd had at my "home" studio in Philadelphia. This dream, however, was so opposed to who I thought myself to be that the voice of doubt rang loudly like reality again. It said, "You don't know how to run a business; you don't even have an associate's degree." It said, "You are horrible with money. You'll never be able to get enough to open a business; let alone keep the business afloat." It said, "You can't do it."

These statements, once again, felt like facts, and I didn't question them until a friend asked me a question: "If you were going to give a group of high school students a talk, what would you say to them?"

I paused and said, "Fear will try to stop you. Go anyway." In hearing my own response, it became clear to me that the "facts" holding me back were the voices of fear and doubt, and I wasn't going to let fear and doubt be the only reasons I didn't do the thing I was most passionate about. That choice changed my life. Within a year, my now business partner Laura and I opened BIG Power Yoga studio.

27

CREATE BOUNDARIES WITH FLOW

Flow is being able to move as you please without any impediment. Proper boundaries help you flow because they exist to help you stay connected to the one essential truth—that you are a divine being. Boundaries are not so much about what you are keeping out but what you are staying connected to.

Boundary setting can help you remain yourself and not have to be someone or something that undermines your highest intentions. As you discover what to say yes and no to, what to engage with and what to ignore, and how close or far to keep people, places, and things in your life, you will have much more freedom to show up as yourself wherever you choose.

For instance, when you feel the need to avoid someone or something, it is likely a sign that you need to set a boundary there. A boundary helps you delineate the difference between who you are and who or what someone or something else is. It is likely that if you are avoiding someone, it is because you feel like something they could do or say could somehow prove something undesirable about you. In reality, there is nothing that can change the truth of your essence. What someone else does or says reflects what they are navigating at this moment, not who or what you are at your core. Boundaries help us remember the truth, and the truth sets us free.

Setting and honoring loving boundaries is a spiritual practice. In fact, the incorrect use of boundaries keeps you closed, blocked, and constrained. Establishing boundaries is not about making yourself superior to someone else or protecting yourself from people you judge or resent. When you confuse your reactionary self-preservation tactics with boundaries, you keep the memories of harmful experiences alive in your body and soul, allowing them to take a little or a lot of your precious life-force energy. You cannot be angry with someone and have love flowing through your body and life at the same time.

If you are committed to feeling more peace and flow in your life and want to have your full personal power to create, then your greatest tool is forgiveness. Practice forgiving and discerning instead of resenting and judging. Practice loving yourself enough to extend compassion and empathy to others so that you don't get stuck with the feeling that comes along with condemnation and unforgiveness. Choosing to stay connected to grace may help you remember that often the best response is no response at all. And the choice to not respond from a place of love is different from the reaction to avoid out of fear. A choice based in love will likely give you a sense of inner knowing and peace in your body because it will feel like an act of service to yourself and others. A "choice" based in fear and avoiding your responsibility will likely create the sensations of tension in your body.

You get to say how you show up, even in the most confronting moments. Enjoying your life is your birthright. Use boundaries to keep you connected to what's essential and help you choose for yourself.

28

FREE YOURSELF FROM THE DRAMA CYCLE

We are the ones who keep the drama in place in our lives, not the other people in the drama. We do this in two ways:

1. **Listening to the small (lower self) voice inside of us. This voice never tells us anything valuable**. Ever. EVER. The only time there is drama in your life is when you are listening to the small voice and giving it your time and attention. The small voice is tricky because it lures you into believing it is valuable by tempting you with goodies like being right, staying safe, and not having to do real work. If you are looking to eliminate drama from your life, you must remember to never believe this voice, no matter what it says about you or anyone else. EVER. When you catch yourself being tricked into believing it, stop it immediately. It can be that simple if you really are willing to let go of the game.

2. **Making it wrong that there is a small voice inside of us.** We each have a small voice inside of us, just like we each have a nose. And just like you have a nose but you are not your nose, you have a small voice but are not your small voice. When you realize a small voice is something

that you just have, just like me and the person next to you, you can stop thinking that you are a bad person or that you did something wrong to have been cursed with doubt. When you realize this, you can make the small voice useful because you know that the more growth and opportunity you experience in your life, the louder that small voice is going to start talking.

The louder the small voice is, the more important it is that you don't listen to it and put even more attention on what you're up to. You can use the volume of the small voice as a helpful hint that what you are up to is valuable. You don't have to freak out and wait for the voice to go away. The voice is never going to go away. In fact, I hope you are up to such big stuff that the voice only gets louder. Learn to let the voice be there without making it wrong.

If you don't want drama in your life, stop valuing the small voice. Don't make it right. Don't make it wrong. Just let it be and do what you came here to do.

29

BELIEVE YOU CAN SO YOU CAN

What you *believe* you can do and what you *can* do have *nothing* to do with one another. What you *believe* you can do and what you *do* have *everything* to do with one another. Here's why.

A belief is not a fact; it's a choice. Yet it is a choice that places real limits on what's possible. Therefore, to begin doing things you never believed you could do, all you need to do is be open to changing your beliefs.

You probably keep your beliefs around because, like all of us, they help you feel comfortable and in control. However, if you want to grow, thrive, and prosper, you have to be willing to be uncomfortable and step into the unknown.

If you believe it, it can be true. If you don't believe it, it will never be true. If you want it, start to believe it. The most useful belief would be to believe you can do anything. From there, you get to choose.

As an experiment, choose not to believe a limiting belief you have about yourself. For example, if you believe you are not an athletic person and this is keeping you from finding a way that you love to stay healthy, do one thing each day for the next thirty days that is in direct opposition to that belief, no matter how true you think it is. If you believe you are bad with money, take one action every day that demonstrates you are great with money. If that feels too far-fetched, take an action that demonstrates you are *learning* to become great with money.

Beliefs are just beliefs, and they can be changed. If you want something new, get to changing yours.

30

LET YOUR IMAGINATION LIGHT THE WAY

Stress often comes from thinking that something we want to be possible isn't possible. Tension arises when the pathway isn't apparent or the goal seems unattainable. Fear keeps spinning us around to face the past. This disorienting or discouraging place of impossibility is a sign that it's time for some imagination.

Roads we have already traveled will only get us places we have already gone. Seeing the new pathway requires the discipline of creativity and an open mind. Our willingness to suspend our attachment to what is probable and actively shift into wonder about what we have not yet done, seen, or been shown helps us reach the new destination. When it comes to getting us somewhere new, our imagination is a much more potent reference than our past-based experiences.

When we find ourselves doubting and limiting what's possible for the future, our work is to let our minds play. We must be disciplined enough to keep what our rational, adult minds "know" out of it. The times when we least feel like imagining are the times it is the most important because imagining is how we restore ourselves to possibility when we want to give up.

Even when we give ourselves permission to imagine, it can take focus and keen observation to truly cross over to a place free from the limitations of the past. To begin an imagination session, you must set some rules for yourself. You must forbid yourself to bring in the editing mind at all, meaning you cannot leave any ideas out simply because they aren't "good" ideas, they haven't worked in the past, they are too small, they are too big, they would cost too much, they are too bold, too silly, too unrelated, etc.

This rule of "no rules" is key. Once you have committed to no rules, you must commit to staying in your imagination session long enough to get to a long pause I like to call "the lull." The lull will occur when your initial outflow of ideas slows down and you feel pulled to stop imagining and get into action. The discipline of holding space and waiting for a second or maybe even third or fourth rush of ideas to come through is the most important part of allowing your creative mind to open. Even if you don't consider yourself a creative person, all you need to do is open up the pathway to be a conduit for ideas to pass through. Once you have allowed yourself the space to experience the world of the imagined, it is likely that you will see many opportunities you had not seen when focused on the past and that your body is energized with possibility.

What you already know will get you what you've already got, and your mind will continue to turn you around to face your past. Your imagination is what will shine the light on the hidden path forward, as many times as you need it, if you are willing to use it.

31

TRANSFORM YOUR "BUTS" TO "ANDS"

But I don't know how.
But I don't have enough money.
But they will say no.
But I don't know what I am doing.
But I don't have the proper education.
But I'm scared.
But I might fail.
But I am not smart enough.
But it's hard.
But I might disappoint my parents/husband/friends/boss/etc.
But I spent money and time on a different education.
But my background is in a different field.
But I will lose my health insurance.
But people might judge me.
But I don't have much time left.
But I've failed in the past.

Your buts will always be there, and you don't have to let them stop you. Having buts is a good sign that you are up to something big. Your buts become louder the more critical your goal, idea, or thought is. Here is the breakthrough idea: your buts are just the beginning.

Way too often, we see buts as an end, when really, they are signals that it is time to more deeply explore and harness our personal power to see possibilities beyond what is obvious. These buts show us it is time to choose the opportunities we would like to bring to fruition. The voice of doubt is sneaky and loves to use the word "but." However, you are wise and know that you are more powerful than the voice of doubt. Let the buts remind you to continue to expand your creative power and freedom.

When you know the buts will be there, they aren't surprising. Instead of being stopped by them, you can expect, notice, and welcome them as opportunities.

32

PRACTICE THIS SMALL THING TO MOVE FORWARD

The thing blocking you from moving into what is next for you could be forgetting to be grateful for where you are.

If you want to move to a new home, first bless and appreciate the one you are in. Spend time in each room of your current living quarters, acknowledging all of the good it has brought you and thanking it for what it has allowed you to do and receive during your time there. As you express gratitude, notice any physiological changes in your body. You may feel a shift even though nothing circumstantially has shifted.

If you want to change the health or shape of your body, first bless and appreciate the miraculous things your body is already doing without you even needing to think about it. Then, just as with your home, spend time with your individual body parts, bringing loving awareness to each one as you go, opening yourself up to being moved by how much you are already receiving from it. Do this practice, especially for the areas you judge or resist.

If you want to find a new job, bless and appreciate your current opportunity. Bless and appreciate each coworker, task, paycheck, and lesson you have learned. Each of these things has been an investment in your future—if you choose to take the time to appreciate and value them. Your gratitude creates the energy and momentum you need to launch into what is next for you. Resentment and resignation build dead weight and magnetically draw you toward what you resent. The great news here is all that is required is a shift in your perspective and what you're saying, and you have everything you need to make that shift.

Being grateful takes awareness and time, yet it is time well spent. The energy created in your body through gratitude will help you feel happier now and simultaneously help you see more opportunities to create what you desire.

33

HAVE A BREAKTHROUGH BY BREAKING THROUGH MEDIOCRITY

While expectations can elevate you above what you may do on your own, they also create a ceiling.

Living a life where you wake up and strive to meet expectations will trap you under a ceiling of mediocrity. This ceiling is problematic because no matter how high it is, your life will never wholly fulfill you if someone else's expectations dictate your actions.

The only way out from underneath this ceiling is to wake up every day and resolve to exceed expectations. Not because you have something to prove but because your creator designed you to help us all grow and evolve together. Setting your focus on exceeding expectations opens up new possibilities that were not available when you were focusing on simply meeting expectations. Committing to exceeding expectations gives you a greater chance of living a fulfilled life. When you exceed expectations, you can make an impact on someone, creating a connection. You can contribute something that changes what others see as possible. This will always be fulfilling for your spirit.

There can be expectations that cause you to rise and transcend your circumstances, such as an expectation to have your thesis turned in on time. On the other hand, some expectations trap you in an old behavior, such as an expectation that you show up late because you always have. Or an expectation that you make poor financial decisions because you have in the past. It is evident how these expectations would keep you low to the ground rather than close to the ceiling.

Whether the expectations you are consciously or unconsciously being driven by are motivating or defeating, they will always be limiting if you don't examine them because true inspiration only comes from authentic choice. Your creator designed you to choose, create, serve, teach, connect, grow, and help others do the same. These things happen when you create the unexpected by exceeding the expectations that can limit your life every day.

The first step to exceeding expectations is to notice how insidious they are. You likely greet people in the way they expect you to, respond to emails in the way your coworkers expect you to, create the small talk people expect you to, do the exercise routines that you expect yourself to do, and the list goes on. To practice shaking things up, begin each day this week by listing three things or more you will likely do today and the expected way you are likely to do them. Then, imagine one to three ways you could exceed your expectations or the expectations of others when you do these things. It could be as simple as the way you make eye contact and connect with someone to as revolutionary as creating a new genre of music. Then, go disrupt the status quo and see what happens.

How would your life change if you shifted your priority from meeting expectations to using expectations merely as a starting point for what's possible?

34

FOCUS ON YOUR PURPOSE AND NOTHING ELSE

Getting other people to like you, agree with you, or understand you is not at all essential to moving toward your dreams. In fact, when you are dreaming big, you will likely stir up the voice of doubt in others who like things to be predictable and stay the same. With this in mind, it is worth considering that when other people in your life voice opinions, that is a sign you are starting to open up to your true potential.

Because the desire for predictability is in almost all of us, and therefore the people in your life, and this want is so strong, there will be times when you will need to choose to listen to yourself and no one else. These moments may feel like the most complicated moments to navigate, but your clarity, not anybody else's, gives you the freedom you have been seeking. You don't have anything to prove to anyone else; you only have to fulfill an agreement with your spirit.

Don't let other people's stuff keep you from living your life. Their reactions and opinions are only an expression of their life experiences and their way of coping with the world. Remember that your happiness, fulfillment, and ultimately your ability to create and contribute great things come from your willingness to trust yourself and move forward. The wonderful news is that you can love people whether they understand you or not. The ingredients to this love are compassion and understanding for those who don't get it and a commitment to protecting your dream.

Their feelings are not your most important priority; your purpose is. Do the thing.

35

OWN YOUR FEMININE LEADERSHIP

We all have feminine and masculine qualities. Some of us have more feminine energy, some more masculine, which isn't dictated by any gender with which we may identify. Both feminine and masculine traits are essential, yet we have lived in a world mainly ruled by masculine energy for centuries. It is time for us all, despite gender identities, to usher some of the more feminine qualities of leadership into our world.

Imagine a world where our governments, schools, businesses, and family leaders listened with acceptance and love, showed empathy and compassion for folks with different viewpoints, and nurtured those in need. Imagine a future where forgiveness allows for peace, curiosity facilitates genuine collaboration, and sharing authentically engenders trust. Envision a planet where people value work in the home and with family as much as work on a computer.

If we can imagine it, we can create it. And it starts with each of us as individuals—especially where it feels the most challenging. You know that person you disagree with and judge? Practice listening to them with agenda-free curiosity—not just now but always. You know the political group that you think your political group is better than? Practice putting yourself in their life experiences and meeting them where they are with the intention of long-term collaboration—not just now but always. You know the folks on the margins in your life and in your society? Spend time with them not to fix them, but to learn from them—not just now but always. What might change within you if you gave yourself the space and time to be more accepting, compassionate, and nurturing? What might this allow for others?

Assertiveness and drive have only gotten us so far. It's time to let balance move us into a new era of love, abundance, and success. It starts with us. You and me, day by day.

Stay in Your Flow
PART 3 JOURNALING PROMPTS

- What is an area of your life where you have not been expressing your loving, best self fully? What if you focused only on how you want to feel as a result of your action, not how the outcome might turn out? What new actions might you take? What might you stop doing?
- Where have you been wishing for something new yet not allowing yourself to devote the time to truly let your imagination reveal some new pathways? Either take the time right now or schedule time to engage in an imagination session to help you uncover new possibilities.
- What is something that you deeply want yet you are letting a "but" stop you? Could you lean into the energy there and begin to imagine how you might do it instead of being stopped by the energy?
- Where are you wishing something else was happening, causing you to forget to be grateful for what you have? Could choosing to feel and express gratitude for what you have right now support you in taking your next step with more ease? How so?
- How are the cultural norms and expectations you navigate limiting you from expressing yourself and contributing at your highest level? What might you do or how might you show up if you were willing to break social norms and be your best, brightest self?

- How do you feel in your body when you are distracted from your purpose and focusing on proving, getting, or placating? How do you feel in your body when you feel you are showing up as your best self and making the difference you seek to make? What sensations will you need to be willing to experience to stay on purpose each day?

- If you become an expert at nurturing, accepting, forgiving, and supporting the people you engage with every day, how might that change the quality of your life? How might it change the results you produce? How might it change the quality of life of the people you care about? How might it change the results they produce?

Part 4

CHOICE IS YOUR SUPERPOWER

In December of 2017, I heard the most incredible news from a doctor of mine. They were the words I had longed to hear for years. They came from my IVF doctor when he called me to tell me I was pregnant.

The excitement of my pregnancy news continued with me throughout my first trimester, even as I experienced nausea, heartburn, exhaustion, and the nervousness and uncertainty of becoming a first-time mother and my husband becoming a first-time father. In fact, I reached the second trimester, and my excitement increased even more as I began to feel better physically. My husband and I had so much fun choosing a name, designing a nursery, and imagining what our baby girl would look and sound like. We were clear about how we wanted our daughter to enter the world, so we planned for a home birth with an incredible midwife.

Yet nothing went as planned. At twenty-five weeks pregnant, I began to experience some lower back pain and what felt like indigestion—normal pregnancy symptoms. I didn't think much of it until my discomfort intensified to pain, and it became clear that I was not experiencing pregnancy symptoms; I was experiencing preterm labor symptoms. My midwife instructed us to head to the best women and children's hospital in town, and my husband and I drove there in silence, knowing that no matter what happened in the next few hours, the subsequent season of our lives would look different than we had planned.

After being admitted to the hospital for monitoring, I was moved to labor, and delivery. The teams at the hospital had tried to stop the labor, but it was clear that our daughter was coming *right now*. As I was rolled to a room with my husband by my side, I was terrified about what I was about to experience, about what the very short-term future (and long-term future, I prayed) held for my daughter, about the heartbreak I might endure, and about so many things I couldn't bring language to. I noticed the fear take over my body and mind, and I felt as though I had no say in what was about to happen. While it was true that I couldn't change the circumstances, I knew that I could make a choice about who I was going to be in response to those circumstances.

I made the decision right then not to let fear take over. I accepted that the fear, doubt, worry, despair, and other emotions I was experiencing were all part of what I was moving through. And while I decided to allow them to be there with me, I reminded myself that they were *not* me. I remembered that even right then, especially right then—in the "now"—I was me. I got to choose how I showed up. I always get to choose how I show up. That choice changed the next few hours, months, and years of my life.

My daughter, Emerson, was born at 6:07 a.m. on Tuesday, May 8, weighing 1 pound, 12 ounces. She was immediately placed on a ventilator and rushed to the NICU. She suffered a grade 4, bilateral bleed in her brain, eventually leading to a diagnosis of hydrocephalus and a series of four brain surgeries. She also endured many of the challenges that so many preemies face; breathing apneas and bradycardias; time on and off CPAPs, nasal cannulas, and respirators; eye surgery for retinopathy of prematurity; difficulties learning to eat and digest; and so much more. To say it was the most challenging time of my life would be an understatement. There were days and nights when we didn't know whether she would make it through, and there were moments when I doubted *my* ability to make it through, emotionally and otherwise. What did get me, and us, through it in the way that we did was the gift of my knowing that I could choose what I focused on, what I had faith in, and who I wanted to be.

I knew that if I maintained my connection to Love, I would be clearheaded for my daughter, making the best possible choices for her and being her greatest advocate. I knew if I came from Love, I would see how to better take care of myself during this time. I knew if I chose Love, I would choose responsibility over worry. I knew if I chose Love, I would make bold requests of others and, at the same time, give compassion and empathy. I knew that even if the worst outcome came to pass—if my daughter did not survive—at least I had spent my time with her on this planet in Love rather than being possessed by fear, doubt, resignation, blame, or any of the other sensations that tried to seep their way in, sometimes hundreds of times a day.

The choice to choose Love again and again was just that: a series of uncountable moments when I had to consciously stop and prioritize what I believed to be helpful over what was tempting. It wasn't easy, but it was simple because I had faith in it.

During our time in the NICU, it felt like we kept receiving the worst possible news and getting hit with detrimental setbacks. Watching my daughter suffer and often not being able to hold her were heartbreaking. I felt isolated, unseen, unheard, and powerless much of the time. While the medical teams were absolutely amazing in their areas of focus, they were often unaligned with each other, leaving the responsibility of integrating the teams and staff to me. I practiced forgiveness and surrender on a daily (maybe minutely) basis.

While I would never wish to go through this experience again or wish it on anyone else, each obstacle was an opportunity for me to expand my ability to show up to life in the vulnerability of both possibility and heartache. I knew that no matter what happened, even if it was not what I wanted or preferred, ultimately, I would not only be okay but stronger because that is how we are designed as human beings.

After a trying four-plus months in the NICU, Emmy was released to come home that September. She was still using an oxygen tank and needed extra care in her feeding. We didn't know what the future would hold as she continued to grow, yet she seemed perfect when we walked out of the doors to the hospital for the first time as a family. We had been warned that Emmy could have conditions like cerebral palsy or developmental issues as a result of her experiences and diagnoses. Yet as the months and years have passed, she has continued to blow us away. She just celebrated her fifth birthday and is one of the most joyful, intelligent, and fun children I have ever met (of course, I am biased!).

The day we walked out of the hospital, I felt grateful my faith had grown rather than faltered. Faith in ourselves or in a higher power does not have to do with everything working out as we planned. Fulfillment does not rely on what happens to us. Our experience of our lives is directly correlated with what we lean on when things get tough and what we focus on when things are beautiful. Our choice, and in particular our choice to Love, is our superpower.

36

DEVELOP A RULE-BREAKING PRACTICE

Each day, we wake up in a sea of beliefs that make up our perspective about our day, ourselves, others, and the world. Some of these beliefs serve us, and some of them don't. If you aren't aware, they're likely not supporting you. My mentor and spiritual teacher, Susanne Conrad, has taught me that what we are unaware of creates more powerfully than what we *are* aware of in our lives.

Our beliefs eventually solidify into limiting rules we use to keep ourselves and others in boxes. For example, if you believe you aren't good with numbers or people, you will likely not let yourself start your dream business. Likewise, suppose you believe you cannot trust people of a particular gender. In that case, you won't allow yourself to develop fulfilling and intimate relationships with people who could contribute to your growth and life.

Merriam-Webster defines a "rule" as "a prescribed guide for conduct or action."[2] But unfortunately, we end up using largely uninvestigated and outdated beliefs as rules that guide and create

---

2 *Merriam-Webster*, "rule (*n.*)," accessed May 23, 2024, https://www.merriam-webster.com/dictionary/rule.

our lives. Sometimes, we know we created a rule that doesn't serve us, yet we need to see that we can make a new choice. The good news is that with discipline and courage, we can.

As human beings who are transforming the status quo, our work is to choose every day and every moment, to notice the beliefs and the rules we are following that no one else is making us obey. If we want to live the lives we are meant to live, it is time to start breaking the rules that keep us small. Once we start breaking these rules, we begin to realize that not only are we okay, but we can also thrive. Systems can be helpful for a time. But our practices should be examined and questioned daily. Who we are becoming today requires something different than we did last year.

If you're ready for the newness and the freedom waiting for you, it's time to make rule-breaking a lifelong practice. Your beliefs can't define you when you don't give them power.

37

YOUR CHOICES AND WHAT THEY CREATE

Your choices create your life. If you feel like more is possible for you, notice the following:

Who are you talking to?

What are you talking about?

What are you watching?

What are you listening to?

What are you thinking about?

Where are you spending your time?

Who are you spending your time with?

What are you using your time for?

These are all things we choose and can therefore change, which can transform our lives. If you feel stuck or are ready for something new, look to these things and see what it's time to upgrade. Brainstorm on each of the following:

What is a dream or a goal you want to start talking about, and who could you talk about it with who would support you and be a resource for you? Examples include starting a business, creating art, learning a new skill, creating a city on the moon, and spending more quality time with your children. Nothing is too big or too small.

Who are some people you could begin to talk with or talk with more who have a positive energy and leave you feeling uplifted?

What could you watch, read, or listen to that would empower and inspire you?

What habitual thoughts can you practice noticing and start saying "no" to? What thoughts is it time to insert in their place?

How could you use your free time to restore or create rather than drain yourself further or consume?

How can you elevate the environments you spend time in to help you live with a better mood and more energy? Which visuals, scents, and sounds could you incorporate that would remind you of who you are becoming?

How might you change your actions so they are aligned with the results you are expecting?

38

CHOOSE WHAT YOU RECEIVE

When we give love to others, we immediately receive the feeling of love. It's how our emotions and physiology work naturally. We don't need to wait for anyone else to provide us with love for us to experience it. Here are some other ways this works:

When we give understanding, we experience understanding.
When we give compassion, we experience compassion.
When we give appreciation, we experience appreciation.
So, of course, when we give anger, we experience it.
When we give jealousy, we experience it.
When we give judgment, we experience it.

We have a choice about what we give and therefore what we receive. If our lives do not fulfill us, we must change what we give. While we have more influence over the circumstances in our lives than we believe, we will certainly never be able to control everything. What we *can* do is ensure that we get what we need by choosing how we respond. Ultimately, it is our purpose to give and receive love, and that flow never has to stop if we continue to choose it. We can choose to unconditionally love the people who challenge us. We can choose to be compassionate and forgiving of the human condition and the mistakes we all make.

We don't need to be friends with, agree with, condone, or trust everyone. In fact, we shouldn't. However, we can disagree with someone and still love them unconditionally. For example, I have political views that differ from those of members of my family, and I love them. If we don't choose love, we are the ones stuck feeling angry and resentful. We can be confronted by our circumstances and still practice acceptance and gratitude. If we don't, we are stuck feeling resistance and frustration. I prefer to experience unconditional love, acceptance, and appreciation over the other options, so this is enough reason to give those things out.

When we set goals or wish for a better future, we are really seeking the experience of fulfillment through experiencing love. We can feel that future right now by choosing what we give and receive. We don't need to wait for a perfect or better future; we don't need to wait until everyone agrees with us or treats us precisely the way we want. Instead, we can choose to give love, understanding, peace, compassion, and acceptance, especially when it seems challenging or even impossible.

Taking responsibility for our own experience is a big undertaking, and there is no more worthy use of our time. Take advantage of the fact that the more loving we are toward others and the world, the more love we experience. It's a pretty awesome deal.

39

CHOOSE TO BELIEVE IN PEACE

Picture peace before you see it. Picture healing before there's evidence. Believe that change can happen. Believe that we can do what has not been done before.

Our actions and, unfortunately, our reactions create the future. Our actions and reactions reflect what we believe. If enough of us think we are doomed, we will create it. If enough of us believe it can be better, we will create it.

What you believe and think about are critical responsibilities you have. If each person became personally responsible for picturing healing and believing in a better way, imagine what we could create. If you think that you don't matter, you do. Each of us counts. Peace starts with you, and we need you.

One of the best ways we can create a picture of peace, healing, and change is to spend time in a visualization meditation. You may find the best time for you to do this practice is in the morning before life gets in your way, but any time of day that works for you is perfect. To start your meditation, find any comfortable seated position, whether on the ground or in a chair, and take deep, slow breaths to help your body relax.

As you deepen your breath and feel your body in the present moment, you may find it useful to let your thinking mind know you don't need its judgment or rationale right now. Once you have given your mind permission to have the next few minutes off, allow yourself to travel to any chosen future time, whether it is the end of your day, ten years from now, or the end of your life, and picture in your mind what it looks like to have 100 percent success, love, joy, peace, health, wealth, love, and happiness there. This moment will be a snapshot in time, so give yourself permission to look around and explore with curiosity. As you allow yourself to see what this peaceful place looks like, there are two essential things to practice. The first is that you let your body feel this experience. This can help you come back to this place throughout your day. The second is to continuously remind your mind that you don't need it right now and then return to this imaginative space. Give yourself anywhere from two to thirty minutes in this visualization practice, and you will notice effortless shifts in your ability to access more peace and clarity.

It takes discipline to keep imagining a picture of success when the world around you is pulling for something else. Your imagination is the greatest tool you have. All we need is for one person to believe it is true for it to be possible. Maybe that one person is you.

40

ALLOW CHOICE IN OTHERS TO EXPERIENCE IT YOURSELF

To release yourself from the need to please others, free others from the need to please you. When you do this, you are also releasing yourself from the need to be satisfied by others. Everybody wins!

You may notice that feeling like you have a genuine choice has disappeared in many areas of your life, whether in your ability to express yourself, how you feel, how you contribute to the world, where you work, how you imagine the future, or who you spend time with. This is not ideal because humans thrive when we have a sense of authentic choice. Therefore, we feel less human in relationships or environments where we must please others, suppress ourselves, and comply. When we feel bound by our roles, labels, or what others expect of us, we forget our innate human ability to choose.

Recovering your freedom to choose and be true to yourself is a simple yet sometimes courageous process to begin. It starts with encouraging and honoring the freedom and choices of others. You don't need people to comply with you, agree with you, or please you. You are already whole, independent of their choices.

However, you don't need to comply with, agree with, or please them either. They are already whole.

Many of us have spent a long time believing that pleasing someone means we respect them. The dismantling of this belief could lead to the great unlearning of our lifetime—unlearning being a fabulous thing. Instead, consider that expressing yourself authentically and allowing others to do the same is the ultimate form of respect. As a "boss" at my businesses and a leader in my communities, I have learned that I feel much more respected when folks come to me with the truth about how they are feeling, what they want, what they see, and what they need, especially when they feel like it might not be something I agree with or would prefer to hear. It feels like the ultimate form of respect to me when people see me as generous enough to hear them, big enough to hold space for different perspectives, and resilient enough to empower change.

When people try to please us, we will always be limited by what we are unable to say and express. Some of the most exciting changes and opportunities in my businesses have come from someone having the courage to share what is in their heart. This experience in being the receiver of authentic communication has taught me the power of communicating authentically myself.

If you find yourself with a desire to begin communicating authentically, a powerful place to start is by sharing what is important to you and acknowledging what is important to the other person. Once these commitments are present, you can elaborate by sharing with the other person what you are feeling in your body and what you are telling yourself in your mind. If this communication comes from a place of total ownership rather than blame, it can lead you down a path of real sharing. Especially if you follow it up with curiosity about the other person.

For example, instead of saying something like, "You never let me do what I want, and it pisses me off," say something such as, "When you said no, I felt tension in my gut, and my whole body got hot. In that moment, my mind told me you always say no to me, and that led to me feeling angry. I know what is important to you is hitting our goals, and I also know that you want to be an inclusive leader. Could you share with me more about why you said no so I can understand more clearly?"

Our true potential lives in our ability to see ourselves and others as powerful enough to be in authentic conversation about the things that are important to us. Does this mean that people will never be disappointed with us? No, it doesn't. Yet our long-term fulfillment comes from knowing that we did the hard thing, and this is where courage comes in. If we can commit to being uncomfortable enough in the short term to let our courage help us create rather than placate, we will no longer feel trapped by people-pleasing because we know the freedom that is available on the other side.

In order to know this freedom in your body over time, you have to be willing to feel uncomfortable things and take action anyway. You must practice doing things that might seem difficult or unpleasant, no matter how you feel about them or what your mind says about them. If you commit to speaking from your heart no matter what, it will eventually be your default choice. And as with everything in this book, this all works when it comes from a foundation of love for ourselves and everyone else. Clarity is a form of love.

41

TAKE YOUR 1,440 OPPORTUNITIES

There are 1,440 minutes in each day, including today. These are 1,440 opportunities to make choices that align with who you are. These are also a lot of minutes to be productive with, yet I'm more interested in you feeling fulfilled than in the number of things you accomplish. When you're focused on only what fulfills you, distractions fall to the wayside, and you'll ultimately be more productive and effective, which is quite fulfilling! If this sounds selfish to you at all, don't worry. The things that truly fulfill you will also be gifts to other people and will become an essential part of the way you serve the world.

The problem is that each day we are assaulted by things that pull us into the past or future. That distracts us from living and thriving in the now. These can be comments from the folks around us that remind us of when we weren't our best selves. These can be social media posts or ads that shift our attention to who we need to be in the future to prove ourselves. These can be rooms or spaces in which we have created our memories. Everything and everyone we interact with can remind us of the past or our perceived future. Much of it triggers us and cues us in subtle and not-so-subtle ways to be a reactive version of ourselves instead of our clearest, most present selves.

This might sound overwhelming, but the point of all this is to learn to use this awareness to our advantage. When we don't know we are being hijacked, we can't shift. But when we understand what it feels like to be taken away from the present moment, we can choose to return to being our best. And this, my friend, is the opportunity of being a human being. We get to choose a fresh start again, and again, and again if we are willing to. We have 1,440 opportunities each day to receive that gift and begin again.

Distractions and reactions don't need to take you out like they used to. Instead, you can notice when you are not your best, give yourself a "take-two" within the same minute, and come back to using your time to do what you came here to do—make a positive difference for yourself and others.

Knowing when you aren't your best is easy. If you don't feel good in your body, if you don't feel proud of what you are saying, and if the voice in your head is not kind to you or others, you aren't at your best. Shifting within a minute takes discipline, and we all have the ability. It takes being more committed to being your best than being right, staying safe, or maintaining the status quo.

Shifting can be challenging. Your lower self will attempt, with all its might, to stop you from making this change, and that is why it takes awareness. Choosing to shift is your full-time job, and it's worth it because you will get your life back. You get to say who you are going to be. Otherwise, you give your choice away.

There are so many simple ways to shift. We are designed to do it! Once you recognize you're not your best, stop and choose a way to shift that works best for you. Some easy ways include taking deep breaths, standing up and moving your body, exercising, getting sunlight, going for a walk, drinking water, saying a favorite mantra or prayer, looking at photographs that remind you of what you love and what you are committed to, journaling, singing, dancing, listening to your favorite playlist, crying, sleeping, getting protein in your system, or watching funny puppy videos (a personal favorite).

Of course, cultivating your own ways is important, and this is just a small list. The thing to remember is that the ways to shift are so simple that they often seem like they can't be the answer. Additionally, our cunning reactive mind likes us to think we can't shift, so it resists doing these things. To get great at shifting, you just need to practice doing it—again, and again, and again. What about putting on your favorite stand-up comedy to break up the energy in an argument or erasing some worry while dancing and singing "Shake It Off" by Taylor Swift?

The good news is you have 1,440 opportunities to start fresh. The "bad" news (or maybe it is good) is you only have 1,440 minutes today to make your difference. Who will you choose to be during each minute?

42

BREAK FREE FROM PRESSURE

What if we didn't *have to* do the things we feel obligated to do?

Obligation, pressure, and expectation are all manufactured. This isn't to say they aren't sometimes useful, but they're simply things humans construct, like your car, phone, and social media. These manufactured things can be helpful, but unfortunately, they can also be harmful and take away our humanity.

We forget that we don't *have to* do the things we often feel obligated to do. We forget that we don't *have to* make a decision or say something just because we feel pressured to do so. We forget that we don't *have to* perform to the expectations of others. We forget because the discomfort of obligation, pressure, or expectation feels so real that we act to get rid of it. The intensity of these sensations can make us feel like we have no choice. We must remember that this isn't true, and we have an option regardless of how loud our bodies or minds are. These things are interpretations, and we don't have to do anything with them if we don't wish.

The tension of obligation, pressure, and expectation can sometimes be helpful. Sometimes, these feelings help us move quickly, honor our word, and create things with and for others. Other times, we may receive undue pressure from others or ourselves to make a choice that isn't right for us. Our ability to choose when to respond to pressure and when to ignore it is what makes us human, just like when we determine whether to use our car, our phone, or an app. The most critical time to do this is when the pressure or the expectation feels so real that it seems we don't have a choice.

When you feel the almost inescapable pressure to please someone or to do something you know you won't be proud of, this is the moment to remember that the obligation isn't absolute. It's made up, and you have a choice. Often, what you need when you feel pressed is space, whether it is space between the truth of who you are and your thoughts and emotions or space between you and the person making a request of you or irritating you.

A few ways you may consider creating space for yourself are taking deep breaths, meditating and observing your thoughts as something separate from you, journaling about what limiting beliefs might keep you feeling stuck, letting someone know you will get back to them after you have had some space to get clear, physically walking away from someone or something, or employing any of the other suggestions in the previous chapter, "Take Your 1,440 Opportunities."

Suffering exists in the human mind, making it malleable. Our work is realizing that we can live where suffering and stress are present and not be controlled by them. You are a human being, and you are free. As we discover our own relationship with perceived pressure, we are responsible for cocreating and letting other people choose too. We are all in this together, and creativity will always be a better path forward than rigidity.

43

CHANGE YOURSELF TO CHANGE YOUR LIFE

My work is to change myself, not anyone else.

My lower self, or my reactive voice that wishes to keep me small, wants to blame someone else when I become frustrated, disappointed, annoyed, or hurt. My lower self also wishes the other person would change and judges them for being where they are.

The problem with this mentality is that when I judge someone and make my reactions their fault, I hurt myself because my judgment and anger disconnect me from my source—not to mention, this behavior is the opposite of what I am committed to. My judgment and frustration block me from experiencing unconditional love and happiness and turn me into the opposite of who I want to be for the other person. When I expect someone to be something they aren't or change in a way that meets *my* expectations, I am setting us both up for failure and abdicating my responsibility and commitment to constantly change and evolve for the better.

The only person who is responsible for changing is me. I am the one who has given my word to it. I am only changing for the better if I become more loving, understanding, resilient, and fun.

For my life to change for the better, I must be the one to change for the better. If I wait for others to change, I will forever be waiting to experience love, understanding, resilience, and fun. Plus, if I don't change, remaining stuck in the past, I won't be able to recognize that others are changing.

Today, I choose to be bigger, better, more loving, more fun, more understanding, more compassionate, freer, and better for the people in my life, not wait for them to be better for me. That's my job because it's what I am committed to. Let your commitment also lead you to something bigger.

44

FIND FREEDOM IN CHANGE

Total freedom is just on the other side of embracing the change in your life.

It's my experience that I get stressed, stuck, worried, or attached when I cling to how things have been in the past. When I think that the past was better, there is no way I can entirely choose what I create now. I can only be in authentic choice when I am fully accepting of, responding to, and grateful for the opportunity right in front of me. Perhaps we are experiencing this resistance because of what we are saying to ourselves. Our language, especially our self-talk, is incredibly powerful and is always creating us. If we want to experience more possibility, it is up to us to speak in a way that helps us see this opportunity. Try saying the following today and any day when change feels like a burden:

"Today, I choose to be completely thrilled about the opportunities and brand-new possibilities in front of me that I wouldn't have gotten to explore unless my circumstances had changed. I remember that without uncertainty, there is no possibility. I choose curiosity over resignation, excitement over fear, courage over doubt, and play over perfection. I have faith in something bigger working in my favor. I am free to create."

You may notice an immediate shift as you speak these words. Or your old, repetitive chatter around change might be so deeply ingrained that it takes some time to become embodied. Either way, practice and repetition are key as our minds will always drift to fear, doubt, and the desire for comfort. The most important part of committing is recommitting.

Change is not only inevitable but also the only way we can get better and grow. Resisting it wastes our energy, keeps us stuck in repeating the past, and has us shrink back and limit our potential for the future. Today, let's remember that the more we embrace change, the more we grow, and the more we can serve.

What is one specific, unpreferred circumstance you could work with today instead of against?

45

CHOOSE THE CHANGE YOU SEEK

Whatever you believe will create your future, so if you're committed to changing for the better, why not have the discipline to choose to see the inconvenient change in front of you as something that can make you better?

If you're seeking to change yourself continuously and positively as part of what you are up to in the world, it's your job to find growth in any change of circumstance.

Change feels tough for us as our bodies and minds are seeking a sense of security through spending time with what we believe we already know. What awaits us on the other side of change is always unknown, and this tends to be stressful for us. Many changes do not seem positive initially, and certainly not all come about because of something sourced from good. Even seemingly beneficial changes that arise from good intentions and a correct place can be confronting for us. The good news is that if we practice being present and noticing the tension, we can make a new choice that can bring more possibility and positive energy flow into our lives.

We can, of course, resist the change and get on board with all the reasons of the voices telling us change is not fair, is not ideal, and all the ways it will negatively impact our future. While this reaction to change is valid and to be expected, especially when we mourn the loss of someone or something we love, staying in resistance won't help us. Allowing ourselves to feel and notice how we feel gives us the power to help ourselves.

We can embrace the change, allowing any number of intense feelings to be a part of the process, and put our energy into a holding space for a new part of ourselves to emerge. We can begin this practice by simply being willing to feel our bodies and notice our thoughts nonjudgmentally. We can do this through meditation, journaling, or simply pausing when we don't feel our best and observing. If we are willing to expand our capacity to feel and notice, we can expand our capacity to embrace change over time. We can only evolve into the next best version of ourselves when we celebrate change and trust that we are designed to grow as a result. If we have faith that our human spirit will transform discomfort into long-term wisdom and joy, we no longer need to fight change.

The imagined future you choose to focus on matters as it will either keep you stuck or help you navigate with a more open heart. You have the opportunity to allow every change to enrich your life and make you more human—if you are willing to feel.

46

CELEBRATE SUNK COSTS

My wonderful business partner used to be a CPA. When we were brand new entrepreneurs, she taught me the term "sunk cost." It instantly became my favorite new phrase as it gave me a mental model for the things I kept around that no longer served me.

A sunk cost is an expense that has already been incurred and cannot be recovered similarly. They should be irrelevant in a decision-making process as they really don't have anything to do with the decision at hand in the present moment. Only relevant costs should be considered. The sunk costs should be written off. This distinction gave me so much freedom because I was living a life full of what felt like constant, low-level burden and guilt.

I had unknowingly been keeping around old, outdated, unuseful emotional clutter of all kinds, simply because I felt guilty that I should have made "better" choices or I didn't want to put in the discomfort of releasing them. I people-pleased so much that I needed to find a use for everything and everyone. I also felt so insecure about my past relationship with finishing things that I felt guilty if I didn't keep going with things past their point of diminishing returns. I was trying to figure out what to do with that half-finished college degree (sunk cost), that old and energy-draining "friendship" (sunk cost), that old furniture (sunk cost), those unfruitful and draining partnerships (sunk costs), and so on. In declaring them as what they were—sunk costs—I could simply let them go and be free to move forward.

I also realized having sunk costs is not a failure; it's an inevitable part of a life well lived. Clearing out the old is integral not only to keeping a tidy physical space but an emotional and spiritual one as well.

The sunk-cost things we keep around require our energy and take the space or attention of other things that could be more valuable. They rob us of our happiness, energy, momentum, and ability to remain unattached. We don't need to do that anymore. Often, the cost of keeping something around or trying to turn something around that we know is not working for us costs way more than it would to get rid of it. To identify any sunk costs that may be impacting your ability to make powerful choices for your life today, get a sense of where you feel burdened, heavy, or stuck, and journal about letting go of those things that no longer serve you. You will sense in your body when you get it. When you identify a sunk cost, appreciate what that thing has given you, how it has benefited you, and what you have learned from it. And then, with gratitude, release it from what is relevant to your choices today.

47

BE SUPPORTED BY THE POWER OF ENOUGH

As I look at my life, I recognize that when I feel stress or uneasiness, it's because I believe there is not enough of something. Whether I am stressed about time, money, love, knowledge, self-worth, worthiness, support, listening, freedom, understanding, or anything else, *lack* is at the heart of the stress.

Not surprisingly, my belief in lack causes me to act in ways that perpetuate the feeling of not enough. However, this is usually because I haven't allowed myself to consider that there *is* enough, that I *am* enough now—not because of any not-good-enough reality. Our beliefs are powerful, and even more powerful when most people share them, which is the case with our societal belief in lack. Our beliefs are so powerful that we will continue to prove whatever we think to be accurate as accurate, even if we don't want it to be.

One of the most harmful effects of beliefs that keep people in suffering is that our long-held viewpoints based in "lacking" keep us from asking good questions. If we believe there are not enough people out there who share our desire for community transformation, we won't ask how we can find the people to collaborate with.

If we believe that there is not enough time to pursue a dream we have, we won't ask how we can create the time.

I would assert that the war, poverty, starvation, political divide, violence, and exhaustion we are experiencing on the planet are a result of our collective belief that there is not enough. So if I want there to be enough food, peace, healing, time, collaboration, and all the other good stuff, which I do—and I assume you do too—I must start believing that there *is* enough so I can access the creativity to help find it. And so should you. You *can* embrace this mindset.

If you want to be enough, you must begin to know at your core that you *are* enough, even when evidence seems like it is showing otherwise. Now, my personal belief shift or yours won't solve our collective communal and global problems, but it's part of getting started and still our responsibility. If we believe there is a fundamental lack of what we need, we must fight for our limitations.

When I believe that *there is enough* to start right now, and *I am enough*, I can begin to make the changes I seek to create. I've noticed that the two phrases "there is not enough" and "there is plenty" produce completely different sensations in my body. The latter boots me up to get to work. Try this yourself by pausing and saying out loud, "There is not enough." What sensations and quality of energy do you notice in your body? Then, say out loud, "There is plenty." What sensations and quality of energy did you notice in your body this time?

Additionally, if you would like to experience the power of asking yourself a question from a space of abundance versus a space of scarcity, journal on the following topics. For bonus points, commit to inquiring about an area where lack feels like an absolute fact.

- What are the moments in your day or areas of your life when you experience the most stress or frustration?
- Is there a belief in a lack that is contributing to that stress? A lack of what (time, money, support, people, agreement, self-worth, etc.)?
- What questions might you begin to ask yourself or others in those areas if you believed there was plenty?
- What possibilities do you see as you ask yourself these questions?

For our world to shift, enough people need to change. I can do my part first by believing in *enough*. Then, I must notice where I am lacking in my actions, plans, thoughts, or what I let myself do or not do. I can then recommit when I need to. When I am enough, *we* are enough, and when *there is enough*, new possibilities emerge.

Choice Is Your Superpower
PART 4 JOURNALING PROMPTS

- Choose an area of your life where you want to feel a certain way or do something new yet you feel blocked. What rules have you placed on yourself that constrict you? What if none of these rules were true? What would you do or allow then?

- Is there an area of your life where you have been waiting for someone else to give you love or understanding so you can experience love yourself? What shifts if you instead love that person now, exactly as they are, or understand that person right now, exactly as they are?

- How do you define success? What societal or familial definitions of success do you accidentally allow to displace your own view of success? How can you refocus on *your* definition of success when you notice this shift happening?

- What beliefs block you from allowing yourself to possibly disappoint others? What beliefs block you from allowing others to express a different perspective or say no to you? What are the life-giving opposites to these beliefs? Would you be willing to try out those new perspectives and see what happens?

- Which activities, thoughts, mindsets, or environments make you stressed, frustrated, or uninspired? How can you eliminate some of those from your day? Who or what might support you in shifting into activities, thoughts, mindsets, or environments that make you feel at ease, whole, and inspired?

- Where in your life are you allowing internal or external pressures to convince you to override your highest values or your purpose? What would it look like to recommit to what feels most aligned for you?

- Locate an area of your life where you are attempting to fix someone else. Instead, what might change in the long term if you focused all your energy on expanding *your* ability to love and create?

- Reflect on a time when you resisted change in your life, yet ultimately, that change opened up something beautiful in your life that wouldn't have unfolded otherwise. What do you wish you had known or remembered during that change? How can you use that wisdom to embrace the opportunities in front of you today?

- Where in your life are changes happening that cause you to imagine a negative future? What is the impact on your life when you imagine these negative things? What are ten positive things that could happen as a result of the changes in your life? How does your body feel when you imagine these positive possibilities instead?

- Which relationships are weighing you down, yet you hold on to them simply because they were a part of your past? Which places are weighing you down, yet you hold on to them simply because they were a part of your past? Which things are weighing you down, yet you hold on to them simply because they were a part of your past? Which ideas, patterns, or beliefs are weighing you down, yet you hold on to them simply because they were a part of your past? If you lovingly let these things go, what would you be able to open up space, energy, and resources for?

Part 5

YOU ARE YOUR OWN FULFILLMENT CENTER

When you order something from a business to be shipped to your home, there is always a chance it will get delayed, canceled, broken, lost, stolen, or end up being disappointing based on what you'd pictured. Any of these things can happen because ultimately, there is very little you can do to control the journey of your parcel. To order something from a fulfillment center means you hand over the power to someone else. And we know that.

We also know that if we want more control over when and how we receive something and the quality of it, we need to be responsible for making it or getting it ourselves. Of course, most of us don't have the time, energy, skill, or commitment to living life this way, so we let Amazon, Wayfair, and Instacart help us out. This release of control over our desires puts the fulfillment in someone else's hands, yet this does not need to be (nor should this be) the case when it comes to your emotional and spiritual fulfillment. In these instances, you are your own fulfillment center.

For millennia, many spiritual traditions have shared best practices for personal happiness and contentment that are not based on external sources but rather on one's connection with the Self or a person's inner spiritual source. The *Bhagavad Gita*, a seven-hundred-verse Hindu scripture (part of the epic *Mahabharata*) teaches us that we find fulfillment when we release our attachments to the results of our actions and focus on the actions themselves. The Bible asks us to cast the burdens we carry onto Jesus Christ and allow him to carry the stress we feel about outcomes so we can be free to be joyful. My spiritual teachers have shown me that our job is to practice personal obedience to our higher Selves by doing what we innately know to do as a result of trusting our intuitive hits or our values. We act from a space of clarity and then release the result, expressing gratitude for the wisdom that helped us see.

If you are anything like me, which I am guessing you are if you have read this far, you were raised either purposely or accidentally to believe that contentment comes from someone or something else; those external forces—not internal—provide happiness. You might believe, as I once did, that you will be happy at some point in the future: once you have found the perfect soulmate, the perfect outfit, the perfect body fat percentage, the perfect social status, the perfect number in the bank account, the *next* perfect soulmate, and so on. With your fulfillment dependent on external things and people, on things that will happen only in the future, how can you possibly find happiness within yourself now?

This ineffective belief system, which I used to hold so dear as well—essentially a *lack* of a thoughtful belief system—keeps us in a perpetual state of dissatisfaction, worry, and fear. It keeps us from taking responsibility for our lives in favor of taking on the role of a victim. Of course, we cannot win this game of waiting until things are exactly right, because nothing is ever perfect, so the wait is always disappointing.

It also turns out we cannot control most of the things we spend our mental energy attempting to control, like what other people might think about us, how they feel, and even what we think and feel. We've spent our time playing a game that we didn't sign up to play, and it is exhausting because we feel like aren't allowed to step out. I am offering a new, better game that also never ends; however, in this improved game, we win all the time instead of losing.

Yes, you *are* your own fulfillment center. Your job is to listen deeply to the wisdom within you and do what you sense is aligned with your highest commitments, and *that's it*. It's a simple job yet not necessarily an easy one, because we have so much to unlearn. However, out of the water, any amount of growth and success on this new internal fulfillment journey will have an emotional and spiritual return on investment that blows the external gratification journey.

We began our journey together in this book with a discovery of Unconditional Love. That was placed first intentionally as it is the breath that gives everything else in this book life. Our unattached action practices will only be fulfilling if we do them from love. Love is, in fact, the thing that gives us the ability to let go. Fear needs us to grip or push. A commitment to love is what gives us the clarity to hear what the next right thing to do is. A commitment to love is what helps us draw upon the courage we need to make new choices. A commitment to love is what keeps us connected to gratitude for the guidance and wisdom of something bigger than our lower personality. Love is what keeps us in control of our own fulfillment no matter the internal or external weather.

I share this as someone who has committed their life to discovering true happiness and helping others do the same. I am not preaching something I have not practiced. The courage to execute on my own inner obedience to loving myself and others has become my lifestyle because it feels so much better in the long run than the alternative. As I trusted myself (sometimes very reluctantly) to move across the country, release the path I had planned, become an entrepreneur, learn to lead and care for others, close businesses, become a mother in an unexpected way, navigate a pandemic and social justice revolution as a business owner and mom, and now write my first book, I have experienced more failure, heartbreak, fear, worry, disappointment, and frustration than I ever could have imagined. There is no way around experiencing these things as a human being.

While the challenges have been significant, and I would not wish to go through most of them a second time, I am now more fulfilled than I could ever have imagined because of what I have learned along the way. I also live a life without what-ifs, regrets, or holding back (for the most part!). I know that I am doing what I am meant to be doing in this season of my life because I make knowing that my priority. If you are willing to make your fulfillment *your* priority and experience big feelings as you discover the power of your own inner obedience, you can also be more satisfied with your life than you ever imagined.

The original proposed title for this section was "Change Yourself. Change the World." If you decide to become your own fulfillment center, everything around you will seem like it changes for the better. The world is full of opportunity when you release the result and trust your divine design.

48

CONTRIBUTE LIKE A PRO

Today (and every day) is a day to contribute. You have the power to make each moment meaningful by doing the generous thing, for yourself or someone else.

By generous, I mean the thing with the most humanity. It could be offering eye contact or a smile, holding a door, picking up the phone to let someone know you love them or see how you can help them, sharing gratitude, lending a listening ear, putting in that little extra planning to make it special, or offering an idea that could be judged in hopes of making a positive change. The moments of connection that you receive and create are what will make your life meaningful. If you want more meaning, contribute more. Your generosity is a renewable resource, and the more you give, the more you will have to give. In fact, it has been shown that one of the few things that can elevate your baseline happiness level over time is being of service to others.[3] So if you want to be happier and therefore have even more energy to elevate the people around you, keep bringing your curious heart to each moment.

---

3   Shawn Achor, *The Happiness Advantage: The Seven Principles of Positive Psychology That Fuel Success and Performance at Work* (New York: Crown Currency, 2010).

Take a moment to envision your upcoming day and the things you will be doing. How could you show up with more humanness and heart, with the intention to make things even just a tiny bit better? The little things are the big things because your life is made up of only a series of moments. Right now is the moment; today is the day.

49

VIBRATE TO CREATE

Your anger or frustration will have the opposite effect that you are likely going for.

Being reactive toward others usually has them back further into their corner. This aggravated behavior is ineffective because when we are in one of the previous states, we are spending energy wanting someone to be different than they are in the moment. We want them to be kind toward us, understand us, hear us, help us, and be on our side. Creating a vibration of frustration or anger does not invite or develop kindness, understanding, or empathy. On the contrary, it almost always causes more frustration and anger in both ourselves and others. The negative energy compounds. The new choice is obvious, and it takes focused awareness and energy.

Of course, responding with what you would like to receive takes not only energy but an extraordinary commitment to leading by example and making a positive impact, even when it's easier not to. If you're reading this, you likely are committed to all these things, so start consciously giving what you would like to receive. You can begin by cultivating a relationship with your body sensations that helps you notice when you are not in a loving or compassionate state. Once you notice this, you can start to use your breath to relax into the moment and create what you want to feel in your body. Keep your awareness on yourself, and be responsible for only you as a way to be of service.

50

TELL HELPFUL STORIES

As human beings, we love telling stories, and we love listening to stories. We're wired that way. We can get hooked, addicted to, and inspired by stories, which can be great when they are helping us be our most energized, positive, creative selves. But unfortunately, illusions created by stories can also be a dangerous thing.

If we know that the people around us are susceptible to being hooked by a good story, then it is our responsibility to be aware of the types of stories we tell. We can tell stories that do good, or we can tell stories that harm. Martin Luther King Jr. was a captivating storyteller; so was Adolf Hitler. One inspired action from possibility while the other motivated action from fear.

Are you telling stories about an inspiring future we can all work toward together? Or are you telling stories to yourself and others about dramas and gossip that keep us stuck in the past? Are you sharing about the inspiring mission of your new business venture or an eye-opening podcast you listened to? Or are you complaining about the traffic on the road this morning, your coworker, or the members of the political party you disagree with? While talking something out so you can get to the other side can be helpful, complaining with no commitment is not.

The nature of stories is that they pull at our emotions, for better or worse. We're emotional beings who are quickly impacted by the feelings we experience. When we experience negative emotions, we tend to put up barriers to possibility and have trouble moving forward. But when we experience positive emotions, we're more easily moved and inspired to come together and work together for something that benefits us all. Imagine being at a family gathering where everyone appreciated each other rather than criticized one another. People would be inspired and excited to get together again instead of bracing for the next encounter.

You have a choice about how you impact people. You are a storyteller by nature. Be conscious of the types of stories you're telling, and you'll make more of a difference than you know.

51

MAKE IT EASY TO CHANGE THE WORLD

Who are the top ten people you interact with most in your life? Grab a paper and pen, and make a list.

Now, what if instead of trying to change the whole world or not even trying because it feels overwhelming and impossible, you focus on making a difference for those ten people through every interaction you have with them? What if you appreciate your significant other for something small they did instead of pointing out something small they *didn't* do? What if you bring curiosity to your children's resistances rather than making them insignificant? What if you pick up the phone to call a close friend to simply show you appreciate them? You can ask them about something important to them instead of texting them or waiting for the perfect time. What if you put yourself in your coworker's shoes and appreciated them for all they do to help you instead of taking their efforts for granted? Make sure to thank them for their hard work. What if you turn your phone off or put it away when you are with your parents, kids, or any other human being? What if you show random acts of kindness to anyone you have in your life and even strangers?

Your kindness, clarity, love, curiosity, empathy, and commitment can change the quality of life for the people you care about. Discover how simple it can be to change the world by asking yourself some of these questions each day and following through on the answers.

If you shift your context of the world, you can flip from being one of eight billion to being one of ten. How does that perception shift your ability to make a difference? You can make yourself and others more significant.

52

EXPAND BEYOND RIGHT OR WRONG

The constant battle between "right" and "wrong" won't cause change. When you're out to prove someone wrong, no transformation can happen. Instead, you become "right," and the other person becomes more "wrong," or vice versa. It's all just more of the same, more me versus you, more division.

To facilitate transformation, you must instead commit to making a difference for the one person in front of you by making them feel more human. You can make this difference sometimes through *what* you say, yet *how* you listen matters more.

Making a difference for the person right in front of you comes from a disciplined, intentional combination of many things: unconditional love; a willingness to feel, learn, and be impacted; nonjudgmental listening; a commitment to responding instead of reacting; self-love; humility; curiosity; directness; the ability to listen for the most helpful question to ask; and a willingness to embrace nonclosure and nonagreement.

For example, instead of listening from a perspective of "When will this be over?" listen and ask, "What is there for me to learn or understand?" Instead of listening from the outlook of "You're wrong," listen from "What truth is present here?" or "What is really going on for this person?" Instead of listening from "I don't get it," listen from "I am human, so I can relate."

The intention of hosting a conversation this way is to facilitate connection rather than produce a winner and a loser. To live in a transformed world, we must each commit to transcending "wrong" and "right," one moment and person at a time.

53

BE IMMUNE TO DIS-COURAGE-MENT

Courage is something we all naturally have within us. It is a gift that can't be taken away, although we can forget we have it.

We practice courage when we do what we seek to do, regardless of fear. We include fear in the process. The more we use our courage, the better we get at it. Of course, some of us are better at it than others due to practice. However, we all have the same amount within us and therefore an opportunity to develop the skill if we want to feel fulfilled.

You get dis-couraged (meaning drained of your courage) when you process the doubts, fears, and judgments of others. These are poisonous things for our spirit, and you aren't designed to ingest them. If you take someone else's doubt, fear, judgment, or a similar unconstructive emotion personally, it will kill off your courage. Believing that someone else's negative reactions have anything to do with your wholeness, wisdom, or potential is how you forget you have courage within you.

The wonderful news is that taking on someone else's stuff is a choice, which means you don't *have* to do it. Instead, you can learn to notice when you are starting to let someone else's issues discourage you by noticing what it feels like in your body when you take on someone else's doubt. For me, I usually notice a heaviness in my chest, a tightness in my jaw, and tension in my stomach. You will discover what it feels like for you. When you notice these sensations are triggering thoughts of changing your mind, or vice versa, this is a moment to reflect and see if you are experiencing someone else's doubt, resignation, or any other reaction.

Remember, being dis-couraged is different than making an authentic choice not to do something. When you are dis-couraged, you're giving your courage away as a reaction to someone else's issues, which is different from listening in and sensing what is best for you. When you make the choice from a wise place to change your mind or opt out, your body will likely feel relaxed yet energized.

Awareness is vital because people are purposely and accidentally dis-couraging you all over the place. It's nothing to be worried about or scared of; it's simply essential to notice so you can choose to own and use your courage. In a world where fear, doubt, judgment, confusion, competition, and greed are rampant, it's more important than ever for you to stay connected to your courage and do the work you came here to do, making your contribution and experiencing the joy of trusting yourself.

In addition, when you use your courage, you permit others to do the same. Using your courage is one of the best ways to support others who have been dis-couraged to see a new possibility. If you can speak up in the meeting, start the business, advocate for someone who would benefit, make the career change, cultivate a new habit, or quit the old one, someone else watching you will see that they can too. We humans are strongly inclined and programmed to do what we have seen before and avoid the discomfort of standing out in a way that could cause people to see us fail or look bad. You can create a picture for others of what it looks like to do something bold and feel the joy that lives on the other side. This will make it easier for others to follow suit because they have seen your daring. Courage is the gift that keeps on giving.

54

LOOK FOR SUPPORT AHEAD, NOT BEHIND

As you work to create something new, it is likely that many, if not most, people you know have not done what you are doing, don't share your commitment, or will feel confronted by the change you are making. These will likely not be the best people to go to for support, inspiration, wisdom, or accountability. In their disconnection, these people may even try to stop you on your path.

Your most reliable source of support is your inner vision and connection to what you know to be true. From there, your work is to find and seek support from the people who have already been moving down their own path of creativity and courage for a while. This is the practice of seeking support from ahead rather than behind.

It's not your job to get everyone to "get it" and support you; that will waste your energy and keep you in proving mode instead of contribution mode. It's your job to find the few who get it and *go*.

55

GENERATE GENEROSITY

Perhaps the most important way to be generous in today's world is to choose to be your best self, especially when it's easier not to be.

It is predictable that today—and every day—you will interact with people who are opinionated, frustrated, annoyed, and set on being right. To be generous means to give more of something (in this case, yourself) than is expected. In the context of encountering those people who might express negative emotions, be generous by choosing to bring your best self to a situation even when the easiest reactive thing to do might be to match their unhelpful emotions. You don't have to agree with someone or even particularly like them to be generous with hem.

At any moment, you have two choices. You can either let the environment (the energy of the people and circumstances around you) impact how you show up, or you can choose to be generous and create a better environment for others. True generosity is a practice and a choice to do the work to produce something unexpected—that's why it's rare.

There are two practices I have found to be extraordinarily powerful when it comes to practicing generosity in this way.

The first is to bring real compassion and curiosity to the conversation or moment. Try to ask yourself what this person might have endured in their life or what they might be afraid of, which could explain their reaction and attitude. What might be their hidden commitments or heartbreaks at the heart of the matter? We don't need to ask these questions directly to change the energy of our listening and therefore the way we show up. Wondering about these deeper roots will likely open you up to ask questions you wouldn't have otherwise asked or to keep listening in a moment you might have interjected or checked out. Generosity is taking the time to understand as best you can what the person is communicating rather than trying to get back to your agenda.

The second technique is to ask the person how you can support them in moving through what they are experiencing, whether it is someone close to you, such as a sibling or a spouse, an acquaintance or coworker, or even a stranger you are meeting for the first time. Often, people simply benefit from you seeing them as whole, their experience being valid and understood, and them being seen as full of potential exactly as they are. They might not need anything from you except to feel valued as a human being. They will likely not know this is what they need, so this is something you can also do without explicitly saying so. Imagine if, in your desire to help someone feel better, you accidentally amplified how powerless they felt or made them more resentful by jumping into the downward spiral with them. This would not help the person restore themselves to their best Self. Instead, you can be a loving space where people can recenter if they choose to by simply offering your compassionate presence.

When you prioritize seeing someone's humanness, you are taking a generous position.

56

DISCOVER YOUR POWER THROUGH STAYING

Often, navigating differing viewpoints gets challenging, and we find we are no longer in a real conversation for cocreation. Instead, we wind up in an often-intense exchange of opinions until someone decides to give in. Then, we go our separate ways, each with our opinions of the other's opinions.

In instances like these, either during or after an exchange, we may quickly interpret any intensity or discomfort in our thoughts or body sensations as being "bad." If we pause and look at the exchange from a different perspective, however, we may start to see the power of a confronting conversation in a new way. Consider that the intensity you feel in the moment is a sign of an opportunity to listen, contribute, and create something extraordinary that breaks a cycle or creates a new pathway for the future. It is easy to misinterpret your feeling of intensity as "run away" when it could be saying, "It's time to stay, open my heart, and make a real difference."

You know from your own experience that when conversations start to push the boundaries of what seems easy and comfortable, usually, someone checks out and leaves, and not always in a way that makes them proud as they are not being kind or understanding to themselves or to you. However, instead of being predictable, you can choose to be extraordinary and stay. The remarkable person (you) can remember that anything new and meaningful created in a family, relationship, community, or organization will require moving through unfamiliar and intense-feeling moments and conversations. The extraordinary person remembers that, often, someone's "no" means "not yet," or "I'm scared," or "I need more information," or "let's work on it a little longer until it's ready," or "maybe there is a different way to fulfill on what's important here." The extraordinary person who stays in the often-difficult conversation remembers that relationships and projects have a natural timing and life of their own because there are so many factors we cannot control, including what needs to be resolved within people and relationships. As an extraordinary person, you can become skilled at setting your agendas aside and listening so what is truly important will be revealed, leading to more flow, cocreation, and closeness.

If you're committed to something bigger than yourself (a relationship, a project, a community, a possibility, etc.), don't bow out only because you are experiencing the intensity of being challenged. The sensation of the challenge is your body letting you know it is time to contribute and create something that hasn't been created before. As a collective, we have yet to tap into what is possible for our communities, families, and the world. It could be that all it takes is your willingness to feel discomfort, the discipline to listen, and the curiosity to understand. We are all more powerful together, and it is vital for us that you stay.

As you explore the practice of staying, you might find that your breath is your best friend. Begin by observing the body sensations and thoughts that arise when a conversation starts to become tense. As you become familiar with these experiences, meet them with your breath as they come up. When you deepen your breath, imagine a picture in your mind's eye of a successful outcome from a higher place. Work backward from this picture by asking yourself what you need to do right now to nudge the conversation in the direction of unconditional love and listening. It could be that you need to ask a new and better question from a space of true curiosity. It could be that what is needed is for you to ask for forgiveness for listening from an attached place. It could be a pause in the conversation until a later date so everyone can restore.

Your breath is your navigation tool. As you feel discomfort or tension, use your breath to help you land both in the moment and in a successful future. Once you are coming from a picture of success, ask yourself what the next best action to take is that will be the most beneficial to you and others. It may be asking another question, creating a commitment for the future, doing something fun, taking a break, bringing some humor, or asking for help. Whatever the answer is, do that thing. Then, repeat the process. If you allow yourself to be present and sense your way into the next best move, you will get somewhere even more enriching than you thought.

57

OWN YOUR STRENGTH THROUGH GENTLENESS

Being gentle requires true multidimensional strength and power. Responding gently and lovingly to yourself and others requires that you use restraint and discernment, practice listening intently, and feel confident in your faith (what you believe to be true). Ultimately, gentleness comes from a commitment to experiencing fulfillment through loving others, not getting others to love you or be any other way than they are.

The opposite of being gentle is acting with force. Force comes from a need to control and override someone else's experience, perspective, or choice because of your own insecurity about your worth and beliefs. Force will sometimes get the job done, yet it does not tend to be fulfilling because it comes from your attachment to your agenda instead of letting love—the highest and best outcome for all—guide you.

Being gentle requires spiritual discipline that is easy to abandon when things seem uncertain or you feel misunderstood because your ancient hardwiring will try to protect you by sending you into defense mode. It's important to remember that treating others and yourself peacefully and lovingly supports you in feeling your best, not winning a right-fight. As I mentioned at the beginning of this book, giving love is the best feeling there is. In choosing love no matter what, you'll create a space where others can feel like themselves around you, also allowing them to be more at ease instead of forceful. They'll know they don't have anything to prove with you.

Imagine your significant other giving you what feels like abrasive feedback about something you feel sensitive or insecure about. As your insecurity is triggered, you lash out by telling them something they did wrong recently and make a snarky comment about what that means about their character or lack thereof. Your partner comes back with a hurtful quip, and the back-and-forth continues until one of you prevails, or realistically, the other person gives up. My guess is that you have been in that cycle before. How did that feel in your body?

Conversely, imagine this person gives you the same feedback, and instead of reacting from your mind right away, you pause to notice the sensations in your body that want you to defend yourself even though your life is not in danger. Imagine you instead use those sensations as a signal to your highest Self that this is an opportunity to give love and make a difference for you and the other person. From there, you say something like, "Thank you for telling me that upsets you. I hear you. How can I support you in feeling better?" Might this type of response open the door for more harmonious communication in the future? Might it allow for a more meaningful conversation about what is really going on? Might it simply release some tension the other person must be feeling? And most importantly, how would *you* feel after responding in that way?

Being gentle and kind is a choice you can make no matter how the other person responds. It isn't a guarantee that things will go well in the context of your desired outcome, but it is a guarantee that you will feel better about yourself. Gentleness allows things to unfold as they are meant to because your defensiveness doesn't create unnecessary resistance, and unfolding can take time. If there is something you are dealing with in your life or a pattern you want to change and taking a position of force is not working, it may be time to try a more loving, gentle approach, starting with yourself.

Some ways to be gentle with yourself include

- sharing with people how you are really feeling rather than feeling like you have something to hide,
- giving yourself permission to learn something brand new without beating yourself up for being awkward,
- forgiving yourself when you react to your children or judge someone walking by,
- forgiving yourself for not forgiving yourself sooner,
- remembering you are a whole and complete divine being under all your human imperfections,
- reading a book, or
- simply resting or taking a nap.

Some ways to be gentle with others include

- giving someone a second chance or a fresh start,
- accepting someone's apology wholeheartedly,

- offering a coworker grace when they are late by giving them a big smile and a deep breath rather than a glare,
- acknowledging that your child or your significant other must be feeling pretty far from themselves to be as reactive as they are being and offering compassion rather than feedback,
- appreciating someone instead of pointing out what they might have done wrong,
- giving your friends space to discover their own lessons in their own time rather than telling them what they should do or feel, or
- asking a question from love and curiosity instead of getting defensive.

Gentleness can be the key that opens the floodgates for love to stream into your world. Practice creating gentleness in your body with your breath, and then express it through your words, listening, actions, and nonactions.

58

TRY OUT THE UPGRADED GOLDEN RULE

Treating others as you want to be treated is most important when the other person isn't around—because you're still around.

The way we speak (or even allow ourselves to think) about people when they aren't around not only unfairly shapes them into whatever we say they are to whomever we are talking to (including ourselves), but it also negatively impacts us as the speaker (or thinker). It's important to remember that just as love is the best feeling there is and we get it by giving it, when we judge something or someone, we become the sensations of judgment and whatever we are judging. When we gossip or complain, we energetically become the aspect, characteristic, or habit we are judging, and that quality becomes more deeply ingrained in us each time we speak about it.

We must also keep in mind that when we gossip or complain about someone else, we double down on shaping them to be what we claim we don't want them to be; this is how powerful our words are. The more we repeat something about someone, the more we believe it, and we human beings are very good at proving whatever we think is true to be "true." When we say someone *is* a certain way, we are robbing them of the possibility to shift how we see them. This is important to recognize because we often gossip or complain about others because we think it will make things better when, really, it sticks those negative things more in place along with making us feel worse in the long run.

If we are truly committed to our own happiness and positive transformation for others, which I know you are, our work is realizing our reactions and opinions about anyone aren't "the truth." Our job is to speak about and treat people with the grace we would like to be treated with, *especially* when they aren't around. This not only gives them the possibility of shifting and changing in your relationship and others seeing them as a possibility rather than a problem waiting to happen, but even more importantly, you will feel better. And when you feel better, that's when you do your best work in the world.

Keeping conversations positive and valuable, especially when we incorrectly think we're being harmless or discreet, takes precise discipline and awareness, which is why we slip up so easily. One of our biggest blocks to feeling more love is the way we allow ourselves to speak about others, both to ourselves and out loud. We've been tricked into thinking the lack of love we sometimes feel is due to others not meeting our expectations, yet it's really about how we treat them and show up for them.

When you notice you want to complain or gossip about someone, try changing the topic entirely to something life-affirming. You could also shift from talking about what they *aren't* to what they *are* that is positive. For example, instead of saying,

"John never gets anything done on time," try, "John is talented at so many things, and his ability to stay in his creative state is a gift he has." Shifting what you are saying doesn't mean you can't ask John how you can work together better to get what you need when you need it, yet any conversation you might want to have will be more productive and positive if it comes from a place of support and admiration rather than judgment and frustration. Everyone will feel better.

See if refraining from speaking negatively about anyone impacts the quality of your life. Inevitably, we will slip up because our negativity bias is real, and our habits are deeply ingrained. Don't beat yourself up about the imperfection of the process because speaking poorly about yourself would undermine the intention of the practice! Be kind with yourself as you learn and expand.

Also, it is worth noting that there are some people and things that are downright evil and harmful. This is where shifting from judgment to discernment is helpful. When you notice yourself slip into condemnation or anger, which takes away your choice, see if you can shift into speaking in a way that allows you to be committed to what you feel is correct yet frees you from the burden of that person's unprocessed issues. It is an art you will cultivate over time.

This practice could be worth trying as an experiment for a day, an hour, or a month. If it doesn't help you feel better and see more possibilities, you will be in the same place you are in right now. Yet if it does work, how awesome would that be?

You Are Your Own Fulfillment Center
PART 5 JOURNALING PROMPTS

- What are five ways you could be more generous with your presence and your love each day? What tends to keep you from being more generous with yourself and your resources? Practice letting those habits be a reminder to be generous instead.

- Where have you consistently been experiencing anger or frustration in your relationships? How might you shift from a reactive to a loving response, potentially allowing the frustration of the other person or people to dissolve over time? How would your life change if you made the choice to react in a loving versus reactive way, time and time again?

- What is the story about the world you have been telling yourself and others? What is a more beautiful story that could inspire you and others into a more creative and loving future?

- How would the quality of your life change if you shifted your focus from pleasing everyone to loving the ten people closest to you to the best of your ability? How would the quality of their lives change?

- Where in your life are you currently spending your energy worrying about being right or wrong? What is a third option you could put your focus on that would help both you and others no matter what?

- Which people, places, or things in your life are attempting to drain you of your courage? What do you need to remember when you notice this happening? Is there any way to eliminate any courage-drainers from your life?
- Where would showing up with generosity be unexpected today? What would it look like to surprise and delight people today by giving more of your presence and humanness than they expect?
- Where have you been avoiding going to the heart of a conversation because it feels unknown, intense, or uncomfortable? What if you were able to seek out and celebrate the unknown, intense, and uncomfortable as an access point to experiencing your love and power? How might that change your life?
- Who in your life do you sense would respond better to more gentleness than you are currently offering them? How so? How might you experience yourself as more powerful if you were gentler with yourself and others?
- Who or what do you find yourself complaining, gossiping, or thinking about negatively on a regular basis? What if every time you noticed yourself doing this, you either switched to a positive sentiment or shifted your focus to a new, life-affirming topic entirely? What would this free you up to do and be?

CONCLUSION

I want to leave you with a handy little summary that weaves together the titles of our five parts and can serve as a reminder of the insights you have gained through your exploration of this book, the journaling you have done, and all you have put into action in your life as a result. That way, if you don't have this book accessible, you can remember these statements or say them when you need to reboot or reinspire. This whole book can be encapsulated by these two simple sentences:

> If you commit to living a life of Unconditional Self-Love, you have already won. You can stay in your flow if you choose to activate your superpower called choice and be the CEO of your own fulfillment center.

As you navigate this great mystery of existence, may you remember that you cannot control other people, so you don't have to worry about that. Instead, you can choose to love yourself and be loving to others as a means of protecting yourself. You cannot worry yourself out of future challenges, so you don't have to spend your precious time doing that. Rather, you can be responsible for your most important resource—your focus.

What you focus on changes the quality of your existence and therefore your contribution. You always have the choice to focus on what has gone wrong, what could go wrong, who has wronged you, or what is wrong with you. However, this type of focus repurposes you from someone who uplifts the world with your essence to someone who burdens the world with your stagnation. As you create your life, you have the possibility of finding meaning and fulfillment every day by focusing on the greatest gift you have been given and the greatest gift you can give: love.

My recommendation is to find something inspiring to be up to with your life, and then go do it with other people. Surrender to creating your life around this purpose, and you will eventually find yourself living every day with meaning, with each thing you do or don't do becoming a part of your greater vision. There is no better teacher than purpose inside of relationship and community. And what you learn, experience, and create as a result will change you and the world for the better, even with the inevitable heartbreaks and challenges along the way.

As you build your intentional life one moment and one choice at a time, remember that the most important part of focusing is refocusing and the most important part of commitment is recommitment. The most important part of love is choosing to give it. The most important part of life is choosing to live it, and your greatest tools for doing so are the intelligence of your body and the wisdom and passion within you.

Also, eat scrumptious food, listen to great music, give lots of hugs, laugh as much as possible, dance, and move your body in ways it loves. These are all essential to doing your part.

Conclusion

If you commit to living a life of Unconditional Self-Love, you've already won. You can stay in your flow if you choose to activate your superpower called choice and be the CEO of your own fulfillment center.

ABOUT THE AUTHOR

Nancy Perry is a wife, mother, entrepreneur, author, leadership coach, and yogi who hailed from Philadelphia before she made her way to Houston, where she gratefully embraced the belief of, "The higher the hair, the closer to God."

Nancy creates organizations, experiences, and writings that curate transformational experiences for people. She is the cofounder of BIG Power Yoga, Live Alive Adventures, and Out Here Yoga. As a Senior Lightyear Leadership Coach, she has had the privilege to share yoga, leadership, and personal development programs in many places and organizations across the globe. Nancy has also been writing a daily blog since 2016, which was the inspiration for this book and provided much of the content. She feels grateful that what she enjoys doing for fun and well-being also generates her livelihood!

Nancy's mission now is to support others in realizing and owning the power and value of their choice and unique purpose. She cherishes personal expression, inclusion, community, serving others, and the combination of play and dedicated work. This is the legacy Nancy is committed to passing on as she supports you in leaving your own chosen legacy. To find out more about Nancy and how to work with her, please visit www.nancyperry.life.

Made in the USA
Thornton, CO
09/09/24 05:20:48

d168a21e-c20d-4e50-9877-5a1740fa2138R02